Fiddler on the Roof

Fiddler on the Roof

Book by **JOSEPH STEIN**

Music by **JERRY BOCK**

Lyrics by **SHELDON HARNICK**

Entire production
directed and choreographed by **JEROME ROBBINS**

Based on Sholom Aleichem's stories

742696

CROWN PUBLISHERS, INC., NEW YORK

to our Fathers

Fiddler on the Roof WAS FIRST PRESENTED BY
HAROLD PRINCE AT THE IMPERIAL THEATRE,
NEW YORK CITY, ON SEPTEMBER 22, 1964, WITH
THE FOLLOWING CAST:

TEVYE, *a dairyman* .... ZERO MOSTEL

GOLDE, *his wife* .... MARIA KARNILOVA

TZEITEL ⎫

HODEL ⎪

CHAVA ⎬ *their daughters* .... ⎧ JOANNA MERLIN

SHPRINTZE ⎪ JULIA MIGENES

BIELKE ⎭ TANYA EVERETT

MARILYN ROGERS

LINDA ROSS

YENTE, *a matchmaker* .... BEATRICE ARTHUR

MOTEL KAMZOIL, *a tailor* .... AUSTIN PENDELTON

SHANDEL, *his mother* .... HELEN VERBIT

PERCHIK, *a student* .... BERT CONVY

LAZAR WOLF, *a butcher* .... MICHAEL GRANGER

MORDCHA, *an innkeeper* .... ZVEE SCOOLER

RABBI .... GLUCK SANDOR

MENDEL, *his son* .... LEONARD FREY

AVRAM, *a bookseller* .... PAUL LIPSON

NAHUM, *a beggar* .... MAURICE EDWARDS

GRANDMA TZEITEL, *Golde's grandmother* ...... SUE BABEL

FRUMA-SARAH, *Lazar Wolf's first wife* ...... CAROL SAWYER

YUSSEL, *a hatter* .... MITCH THOMAS

CONSTABLE .... JOSEPH SULLIVAN
FYEDKA, *a young man* .... JOE PONAZECKI
SASHA, *his friend* .... ROBERT BERDEEN

and

THE FIDDLER .... GINO CONFORTI

VILLAGERS .... TOM ABBOTT, JOHN C. ATTLE, SUE BABEL, SAMMY BAYES, ROBERT BERDEEN, LORENZO BIANCO, DUANE BODIN, ROBERT CURRIE, SARAH FELCHER, TONY GARDELL, LOUIS GENEVRINO, ROSS GIFFORD, DAN JASIN, SANDRA KAZAN, THOM KOUTSOUKOS, SHARON LERIT, SYLVIA MANN, PEFF MODELSKI, IRENE PARIS, CHARLES RULE, CAROL SAWYER, ROBERTA SENN, MITCH THOMAS, HELEN VERBIT

Entire production directed and choreographed by JEROME ROBBINS. Settings by BORIS ARONSON. Costumes by PATRICIA ZIPPRODT. Lighting by JEAN ROSENTHAL. Orchestrations by DON WALKER. Musical Direction and Vocal Arrangements by MILTON GREENE. Dance Music arranged by BETTY WALBERG. Production Stage Manager, RUTH MITCHELL. Produced by special permission of the Estate of Olga Rabinowitz, Arnold Perl, and Crown Publishers, Inc.

The place: Anatevka, a village in Russia.

The time: 1905, on the eve of the revolutionary period.

ACT ONE

PROLOGUE

The exterior of TEVYE'S *house. A* FIDDLER *is seated on the roof, playing.* TEVYE *is outside the house.*

TEVYE

A fiddler on the roof. Sounds crazy, no? But in our little village of Anatevka, you might say every one of us is a fiddler on the roof, trying to scratch out a pleasant, simple tune without breaking his neck. It isn't easy. You may ask, why do we stay up here if it's so dangerous? We stay because Anatevka is our home. And how do we keep our balance? That I can tell you in a word — tradition!

VILLAGERS

(Enter, singing.)
Tradition, tradition — Tradition.
Tradition, tradition — Tradition.

TEVYE

Because of our traditions, we've kept our balance for many, many years. Here in Anatevka we have traditions for everything — how to eat, how to sleep, how to wear clothes. For instance, we always keep our heads covered and always wear a little prayer shawl. This shows our constant devotion to God. You may ask, how did this tradition start? I'll tell you — I don't know! But it's a tradition. Because of our traditions, everyone knows who he is and what God expects him to do.

1

TEVYE *and* PAPAS
(Sing)

["Tradition"]

Who, day and night,
Must scramble for a living,
Feed a wife and children,
Say his daily prayers?
And who has the right,
As master of the house,
To have the final word at home?

ALL

The papa, the papa — Tradition.
The papa, the papa — Tradition.

GOLDE *and* MAMAS

Who must know the way to make a proper home,
A quiet home, a kosher home?
Who must raise a family and run the home
So Papa's free to read the Holy Book?

ALL

The mama, the mama — Tradition.
The mama, the mama — Tradition.

SONS

At three I started Hebrew school,
At ten I learned a trade.
I hear they picked a bride for me.
I hope she's pretty.

ALL

The sons, the sons — Tradition.
The sons, the sons — Tradition.

DAUGHTERS

And who does Mama teach

To mend and tend and fix,
Preparing me to marry
Whoever Papa picks?

ALL

The daughters, the daughters — Tradition.
The daughters, the daughters — Tradition.

(*They repeat the song as a round.*)

PAPAS

The papas.

MAMAS

The mamas.

SONS

The sons.

DAUGHTERS

The daughters.

ALL

Tradition.

PAPAS

The papas.

MAMAS

The mamas.

SONS

The sons.

DAUGHTERS

The daughters.

ALL

Tradition.

TEVYE

And in the circle of our little village, we have always had our
special types. For instance, Yente, the matchmaker . . .

YENTE

Avram, I have a perfect match for your son. A wonderful girl.

AVRAM

Who is it?

YENTE

Ruchel, the shoemaker's daughter.

AVRAM

Ruchel? But she can hardly see. She's almost blind.

YENTE

Tell the truth, Avram, is your son so much to look at? The way she sees and the way he looks, it's a perfect match.

(*All dance.*)

TEVYE

And Reb Nahum, the beggar . . .

NAHUM

Alms for the poor, alms for the poor.

LAZAR

Here, Reb Nahum, is one kopek.

NAHUM

One kopek? Last week you gave me two kopeks.

LAZAR

I had a bad week.

NAHUM

So if you had a bad week, why should I suffer?

(*All dance.*)

TEVYE

And, most important, our beloved rabbi . . .

MENDEL

Rabbi, may I ask you a question?

RABBI

Certainly, my son.

MENDEL

Is there a proper blessing for the Tsar?

4

A blessing for the Tsar? Of course. May God bless and keep the Tsar — far away from us!

(*All dance.*)

TEVYE

Then, there are the others in our village. They make a much bigger circle.

(*The* PRIEST, *the* CONSTABLE, *and other* RUSSIANS *cross the stage. The two groups nod to each other.*)

TEVYE

His Honor the Constable, his Honor the Priest, and his Honor — many others. We don't bother them, and, so far, they don't bother us. And among ourselves we get along perfectly well. Of course, there was the time (*pointing to the* TWO MEN) when he sold him a horse and he delivered a mule, but that's all settled now. Now we live in simple peace and harmony and —

(*The* TWO MEN *begin an argument, which is taken up by the entire group.*)

FIRST MAN

It was a horse.

SECOND MAN

It was a mule.

FIRST MAN

It was a horse!

SECOND MAN

It was a mule, I tell you!

VILLAGERS

Horse!

VILLAGERS

Mule!

5

VILLAGERS
Horse!

VILLAGERS
Mule!

VILLAGERS
Horse!

VILLAGERS
Mule!

VILLAGERS
Horse!

VILLAGERS
Mule!

EVERYONE
Tradition, tradition — Tradition.
Tradition, tradition — Tradition.

TEVYE
(*Quieting them*)
Tradition. Without our traditions, our lives would be as shaky
as — as a fiddler on the roof!

(*The* VILLAGERS *exit, and the house
opens to show its interior.*)

SCENE ONE

The kitchen of TEVYE's *house.* GOLDE, TZEITEL, *and* HODEL
are preparing for the Sabbath. SPHRINTZE *and* BIELKE *enter from
outside, carrying logs.*

SHPRINTZE
Mama, where should we put these?

GOLDE
Put them on my head! By the stove, foolish girl. Where is
Chava?

6

HODEL

She's in the barn, milking.

BIELKE

When will Papa be home?

GOLDE

It's almost Sabbath and he worries a lot when he'll be home!
All day long riding on top of his wagon like a prince.

TZEITEL

Mama, you know that Papa works hard.

GOLDE

His horse works harder! And you don't have to defend your
papa to me. I know him a little longer than you. He could
drive a person crazy. (*Under her breath.*) He should only
live and be well. (*Out loud.*) Shprintze, bring me some more
potatoes.

> (CHAVA *enters, carrying a basket,*
> *with a book under her apron.*)

Chava, did you finish milking?

CHAVA

Yes, Mama. (*She drops the book.*)

GOLDE

You were reading again? Why does a girl have to read? Will
it get her a better husband? Here. (*Hands* CHAVA *the book.*)

> (CHAVA *exits into the house.* SHPRINTZE
> *enters with basket of potatoes.*)

SHPRINTZE

Mama, Yente's coming. She's down the road.

HODEL

Maybe she's finally found a good match for you, Tzeitel.

GOLDE

From your mouth to God's ears.

7

TZEITEL

Why does she have to come now? It's almost Sabbath.

GOLDE

Go finish in the barn. I want to talk to Yente alone.

SHPRINTZE

Mama, can I go out and play?

GOLDE

You have feet? Go.

BIELKE

Can I go too?

GOLDE

Go too.

(SHPRINTZE *and* BIELKE *exit.*)

TZEITEL

But Mama, the men she finds. The last one was so old and he was bald. He had no hair.

GOLDE

A poor girl without a dowry can't be so particular. You want hair, marry a monkey.

TZEITEL

After all, Mama, I'm not yet twenty years old, and —

GOLDE

Shah! (*Spits between her fingers.*) Do you have to boast about your age? Do you want to tempt the Evil Eye? Inside.

(TZEITEL *leaves the kitchen as* YENTE *enters from outside.*)

YENTE

Golde darling, I had to see you because I have such news for you. And not just every-day-in-the-week news — once-in-a-lifetime news. And where are your daughters? Outside, no?

Good. Such diamonds, such jewels. You'll see, Golde, I'll find every one of them a husband. But you shouldn't be so picky. Even the worst husband, God forbid, is better than no husband, God forbid. And who should know better than me? Ever since my husband died I've been a poor widow, alone, nobody to talk to, nothing to say to anyone. It's no life. All I do at night is think of him, and even thinking of him gives me no pleasure, because you know as well as I, he was not much of a person. Never made a living, everything he touched turned to mud, but better than nothing.

MOTEL

(*Entering*)

Good evening. Is Tzeitel in the house?

GOLDE

But she's busy. You can come back later.

MOTEL

There's something I'd like to tell her.

GOLDE

Later.

TZEITEL

(*Entering*)

Oh, Motel, I thought I heard you.

GOLDE

Finish what you were doing. (TZEITEL *goes out.* To MOTEL) I said later.

MOTEL

(*Exiting*)

All right!

YENTE

What does that poor little tailor, Motel, want with Tzeitel?

GOLDE

They have been friends since they were babies together. They talk, they play . . .

9

YENTE
(*Suspiciously*)
They play? What do they play?

GOLDE
Who knows? They're just children.

YENTE
From such children, come other children.

GOLDE
Motel, he's a nothing. Yente, you said —

YENTE
Ah, children, children! They are your blessing in your old age. But my Aaron, may he rest in peace, couldn't give me children. Believe me, he was good as gold, never raised his voice to me, but otherwise he was not much of a man, so what good is it if he never raised his voice? But what's the use complaining. Other women enjoy complaining, but not Yente. Not every woman in the world is a Yente. Well, I must prepare my poor Sabbath table, so goodbye, Golde, and it was a pleasure talking our hearts out to each other. (*She starts to exit.*)

GOLDE
Yente, you said you had news for me.

YENTE
(*Returning*)
Oh, I'm losing my head. One day it will fall off altogether, and a horse will kick it into the mud, and goodbye, Yente. Of course, the news. It's about Lazar Wolf, the butcher. A good man, a fine man. And I don't have to tell you that he's well off. But he's lonely, the poor man. After all, a widower . . . You understand? Of course you do. To make it short, out of the whole town, he's cast his eye on Tzeitel.

GOLDE
My Tzeitel?

10

YENTE

No, the Tsar's Tzeitel! Of course your Tzeitel.

GOLDE

Such a match, for my Tzeitel. But Tevye wants a learned man. He doesn't like Lazar.

YENTE

Fine. So he won't marry him. Lazar wants the daughter, not the father. Listen to me, Golde, send Tevye to him. Don't tell him what it's about. Let Lazar discuss it himself. He'll win him over. He's a good man, a wealthy man — true? Of course true! So you'll tell me how it went, and you don't have to thank me, Golde, because aside from my fee — which anyway Lazar will pay — it gives me satisfaction to make people happy — what better satisfaction is there? So goodbye, Golde, and you're welcome.

(*She goes out. Enter* TZEITEL.)

TZEITEL

What did she want, Mama?

GOLDE

When I want you to know, I'll tell you. Finish washing the floor.

(*She exits.* HODEL *and* CHAVA *enter with wash mop and bucket.*)

HODEL

I wonder if Yente found a husband for you?

TZEITEL

I'm not anxious for Yente to find me a husband.

CHAVA

(*Teasing*)

Not unless it's Motel, the tailor.

TZEITEL

I didn't ask you.

11

HODEL

Tzeitel, you're the oldest. They have to make a match for you before they can make one for me.

CHAVA

And then after her, one for me.

HODEL

So if Yente brings —

TZEITEL

Oh, Yente! Yente!

HODEL

Well, somebody has to arrange the matches. Young people can't decide these things for themselves.

CHAVA

She might bring someone wonderful —

HODEL

Someone interesting —

CHAVA

And well off —

HODEL

And important —

["Matchmaker, Matchmaker"]

Matchmaker, Matchmaker,
Make me a match,
Find me a catch.
Catch me a catch.
Matchmaker, Matchmaker,
Look through your book
And make me a perfect match.

CHAVA

Matchmaker, Matchmaker,
I'll bring the veil,
You bring the groom,

12

Slender and pale.
Bring me a ring for I'm longing to be
The envy of all I see.

HODEL

For Papa,
Make him a scholar.

CHAVA

For Mama,
Make him rich as a king.

CHAVA *and* HODEL

For me, well,
I wouldn't holler
If he were as handsome as anything.

Matchmaker, Matchmaker,
Make me a match,
Find me a find,
Catch me a catch.
Night after night in the dark I'm alone,
So find me a match
Of my own.

TZEITEL

Since when are you interested in a match, Chava? I thought
you just had your eye on your books. (HODEL *chuckles.*) And
you have your eye on the rabbi's son.

HODEL

Why not? We only have one rabbi and he only has one son.
Why shouldn't I want the best?

TZEITEL

Because you're a girl from a poor family. So whatever Yente
brings, you'll take. Right? Of course right. (*Sings.*)

Hodel, oh Hodel,
Have I made a match for you!

13

He's handsome, he's young!
All right, he's sixty-two,
But he's a nice man, a good catch — true? True.

I promise you'll be happy.
And even if you're not,
There's more to life than that —
Don't ask me what.

Chava, I found him.
Will you be a lucky bride!
He's handsome, he's tall —
That is, from side to side.
But he's a nice man, a good catch — right? Right.

You heard he has a temper.
He'll beat you every night,
But only when he's sober,
So you're all right.

Did you think you'd get a prince?
Well, I do the best I can.
With no dowry, no money, no family background
Be glad you got a man.

CHAVA

Matchmaker, Matchmaker,
You know that I'm
Still very young.
Please, take your time.

HODEL

Up to this minute
I misunderstood
That I could get stuck for good.

14

CHAVA *and* HODEL
Dear Yente,
See that he's gentle.
Remember,
You were also a bride.
It's not that
I'm sentimental.
CHAVA, HODEL, *and* TZEITEL
It's just that I'm terrified!

Matchmaker, Matchmaker,
Plan me no plans,
I'm in no rush.
Maybe I've learned
Playing with matches
A girl can get burned.
So,
Bring me no ring,
Groom me no groom,
Find me no find,
Catch me no catch,
Unless he's a matchless match.

SCENE TWO

The exterior of TEVYE's *house.* TEVYE *enters, pulling his cart. He stops, and sits on the wagon seat, exhausted.*

TEVYE

Today I am a horse. Dear God, did you have to make my poor old horse lose his shoe just before the Sabbath? That wasn't nice. It's enough you pick on me, Tevye, bless me with five daughters, a life of poverty. What have you got against my horse? Sometimes I think when things are too quiet up there,

15

You say to Yourself: "Let's see, what kind of mischief can I play on my friend Tevye?"

(*Entering from house*)
You're finally here, my breadwinner.

TEVYE
(*To heaven*)
I'll talk to You later.

GOLDE

Where's your horse?

TEVYE
He was invited to the blacksmith's for the Sabbath.

GOLDE
Hurry up, the sun won't wait for you. I have something to say to you. (*Exits into the house.*)

TEVYE
As the Good Book says, "Heal us, O Lord, and we shall be healed." In other words, send us the cure, we've got the sickness already. (*Gestures to the door.*) I'm not really complaining — after all, with Your help, I'm starving to death. You made many, many poor people. I realize, of course, that it's no shame to be poor, but it's no great honor either. So what would have been so terrible if I had a small fortune?

["If I Were a Rich Man"]

If I were a rich man
Daidle deedle daidle
Digguh digguh deedle daidle dum,
All day long I'd biddy biddy bum,
If I were a wealthy man.

Wouldn't have to work hard,
Daidle deedle daidle

16

Digguh digguh deedle daidle dum,
If I were a biddy biddy rich
Digguh digguh deedle daidle man.

I'd build a big, tall house with rooms by the dozen
Right in the middle of the town,
A fine tin roof and real wooden floors below.
There would be one long staircase just going up,
And one even longer coming down,
And one more leading nowhere just for show.

I'd fill my yard with chicks and turkeys and geese
And ducks for the town to see and hear,
Squawking just as noisily as they can.
And each loud quack and cluck and gobble and honk
Will land like a trumpet on the ear,
As if to say, here lives a wealthy man.
(*Sighs.*)

If I were a rich man,
Daidle deedle daidle
Digguh digguh deedle daidle dum,
All day long I'd biddy biddy bum,
If I were a wealthy man.

Wouldn't have to work hard,
Daidle deedle daidle
Digguh digguh deedle daidle dum,
If I were a biddy biddy rich
Digguh digguh deedle daidle man.

I see my wife, my Golde, looking like a rich man's wife,
With a proper double chin,
Supervising meals to her heart's delight.
I see her putting on airs and strutting like a peacock,

Oi! what a happy mood she's in,
Screaming at the servants day and night.

The most important men in town will come to fawn on me.
They will ask me to advise them like a Solomon the Wise,
"If you please, Reb Tevye. Pardon me, Reb Tevye,"
Posing problems that would cross a rabbi's eyes.
(*He chants.*)

And it won't make one bit of diff'rence
If I answer right or wrong.
When you're rich they think you really know!

If I were rich I'd have the time that I lack
To sit in the synagogue and pray,
And maybe have a seat by the eastern wall,
And I'd discuss the Holy Books with the learned men
Seven hours every day.
That would be the sweetest thing of all.
(*Sighs.*)

If I were a rich man,
Daidle deedle daidle
Digguh digguh deedle daidle dum,
All day long I'd biddy biddy bum,
If I were a wealthy man.

Wouldn't have to work hard,
Daidle deedle daidle
Digguh digguh deedle daidle dum,
Lord, who made the lion and the lamb,
You decreed I should be what I am,
Would it spoil some vast, eternal plan —
If I were a wealthy man?

(*As the song ends,* MORDCHA, MENDEL, PERCHIK,
AVRAM, *and other* TOWNSPEOPLE *enter.*)

18

MORDCHA

There he is! You forgot my order for the Sabbath!

TEVYE

Reb Mordcha, I had a little accident with my horse.

MENDEL

Tevye, you didn't bring the Rabbi's order.

TEVYE

I know, Reb Mendel.

AVRAM

Tevye, you forgot my order for the Sabbath.

TEVYE

This is bigger news than the plague in Odessa.

AVRAM

(*Waving the newspaper that he holds*)

Talking about news, terrible news in the outside world — terrible!

MORDCHA

What is it?

MENDEL

What does it say?

AVRAM

In a village called Rajanka, all the Jews were evicted, forced to leave their homes.

(*They all look at each other.*)

MENDEL

For what reason?

AVRAM

It doesn't say. Maybe the Tsar wanted their land. Maybe a plague . . .

MORDCHA

May the Tsar have his own personal plague.

ALL

Amen.

MENDEL
(*To* AVRAM)
Why don't you ever bring us some good news?

AVRAM
I only read it. It was an edict from the authorities.

MORDCHA
May the authorities start itching in places that they can't reach.

ALL
Amen.

PERCHIK
(*Has quietly entered during above and sat down to rest.*)
Why do you curse them? What good does your cursing do? You stand around and curse and chatter and don't do anything, You'll all chatter your way into the grave.

MENDEL
Excuse me, you're not from this village.

PERCHIK
No.

MENDEL
And where are you from?

PERCHIK
Kiev. I was a student in the university there.

MORDCHA
Aha! The university. Is that where you learned to criticize your elders?

PERCHIK
That's where I learned that there is more to life than talk. You should know what's going on in the outside world.

MORDCHA
Why should I break my head about the outside world? Let them break their own heads.

TEVYE

He's right. As the Good Book says, "If you spit in the air, it lands in your face."

PERCHIK

That's nonsense. You can't close your eyes to what's happening in the world.

TEVYE

He's right.

AVRAM

He's right and he's right? How can they both be right?

TEVYE

You know, you're also right.

MORDCHA

He's right! He's still wet behind the ears! Good Sabbath, Tevye.

VILLAGERS

Good Sabbath, Tevye.

(*They take their orders and leave.* MENDEL *remains.*)

MENDEL

Tevye, the rabbi's order. My cheese!

TEVYE

Of course. So you're from Kiev, Reb . . .

PERCHIK

Perchik.

TEVYE

Perchik. So, you're a newcomer here. As Abraham said, "I am a stranger in a strange land."

MENDEL

Moses said that.

TEVYE

(*To* MENDEL)

Forgive me. As King David put it, "I am slow of speech and slow of tongue."

21

MENDEL

That was also Moses.

TEVYE

For a man with a slow tongue, he talked a lot.

MENDEL

And the cheese!

(TEVYE *notices that* PERCHIK
is eying the cheese hungrily.)

TEVYE

Here, have a piece.

PERCHIK

I have no money. And I am not a beggar.

TEVYE

Here — it's a blessing for me to give.

PERCHIK

Very well — for your sake! (*He takes the cheese and devours it.*)

TEVYE

Thank you. You know, it's no crime to be poor.

PERCHIK

In this world, it's the rich who are the criminals. Some day
their wealth will be ours.

TEVYE

That would be nice. If they would agree, I would agree.

MENDEL

And who will make this miracle come to pass?

PERCHIK

People. Ordinary people.

MENDEL

Like you?

PERCHIK

Like me.

22

Zero Mostel addresses Heaven

Zero Mostel as Tevye

MENDEL

Nonsense!

TEVYE

And until your golden day comes, Reb Perchik, how will you live?

PERCHIK

By giving lessons to children. Do you have children?

TEVYE

I have five daughters.

PERCHIK

Five?

TEVYE

Daughters.

PERCHIK

Girls should learn too. Girls are people.

MENDEL

A radical!

PERCHIK

I would be willing to teach them. Open their minds to great thoughts.

TEVYE

What great thoughts?

PERCHIK

Well, the Bible has many lessons for our times.

TEVYE

I am a very poor man. Food for lessons? (PERCHIK *nods*.) Good. Stay with us for the Sabbath. Of course, we don't eat like kings, but we don't starve, either. As the Good Book says, "When a poor man eats a chicken, one of them is sick."

MENDEL

Where does the Book say that?

TEVYE

Well, it doesn't exactly say that, but someplace it has something about a chicken. Good Sabbath.

MENDEL
Good Sabbath.

PERCHIK

Good Sabbath.

(MENDEL *exits as* TEVYE *and* PERCHIK *enter the house.*)

SCENE THREE

The interior of TEVYE's *house.* TEVYE's *daughters are there.* TEVYE *and* PERCHIK *enter.*

TEVYE

Good Sabbath, children.

DAUGHTERS
(*Running to him*)

Good Sabbath, Papa.

TEVYE

Children! (*They all stop.*) This is Perchik. Perchik, this is my oldest daughter.

PERCHIK

Good Sabbath.

TZEITEL

Good Sabbath.

PERCHIK

You have a pleasant daughter.

TEVYE

I have five pleasant daughters. (*He beckons to the girls, and they run into his arms, eagerly, and* TEVYE *kisses each.*) This is mine . . . this is mine . . . this is mine . . . this is mine . . . this is mine . . .

(MOTEL *enters.* TEVYE *almost kisses him in sequence.*)

This is not mine. Perchik, this is Motel Kamzoil and he is —

24

GOLDE
(Entering)

So you did me a favor and came in.

TEVYE

This is also mine. Golde, this is Perchik, from Kiev, and he is staying the Sabbath with us. He is a teacher. (*To* SHPRINTZE *and* BIELKE) Would you like to take lessons from him? (*They giggle.*)

PERCHIK

I am really a good teacher, a very good teacher.

HODEL

I heard once, the rabbi who must praise himself has a congregation of one.

PERCHIK

Your daughter has a quick and witty tongue.

TEVYE

The wit she gets from me. As the Good Book says —

GOLDE

The Good Book can wait. Get washed!

TEVYE

The tongue she gets from her mother.

GOLDE

Motel, you're also eating with us? (MOTEL *gestures, "Yes, if I may."*) Of course, another blessing. Tzeitel, two more. Shprintze, Bielke, get washed. Get the table.

TZEITEL

Motel can help me.

GOLDE

All right. Chava, you go too. (*To* PERCHIK) You can wash outside at the well.

(Exit the DAUGHTERS, PERCHIK, *and* MOTEL.)

Tevye, I have something to say to you.

25

TEVYE

Why should today be different? (*He starts to pray.*)

GOLDE

Tevye, I have to tell you —

TEVYE

Shhh. I'm praying. (*Prays.*)

GOLDE

(*Having waited a moment*)

Lazar Wolf wants to see you.

(TEVYE *begins praying again, stopping only to respond to* GOLDE, *then returning to prayer.*)

TEVYE

The butcher? About what? (*Prays.*)

GOLDE

I don't know. Only that he says it is important.

TEVYE

What can be important? I have nothing for him to slaughter. (*Prays.*)

GOLDE

After the Sabbath, see him and talk to him.

TEVYE

Talk to him about what? If he is thinking about buying my new milk cow (*prays*) he can forget it. (*Prays.*)

GOLDE

Tevye, don't be an ox. A man sends an important message, at least you can talk to him.

TEVYE

Talk about what? He wants my new milk cow! (*Prays.*)

GOLDE

(*Insisting*)

Talk to him!

26

TEVYE

All right. After the Sabbath, I'll talk to him.

>(TEVYE *and* GOLDE *exit. He is still
>praying.* MOTEL, TZEITEL, *and* CHAVA
>*bring in the table.* CHAVA *exits.*)

TZEITEL

Motel, Yente was here.

MOTEL

I saw her.

TZEITEL

If they agree on someone, there will be a match and then it
will be too late for us.

MOTEL

Don't worry, Tzeitel. I have found someone who will sell me
his used sewing machine, so in a few weeks I'll have saved up
enough to buy it, and then your father will be impressed with
me and . . .

TZEITEL

But, Motel, a few weeks may be too late.

MOTEL

But what else can we do?

TZEITEL

You could ask my father for my hand tonight. Now!

MOTEL

Why should he consider me now? I'm only a poor tailor.

TZEITEL

And I'm only the daughter of a poor milkman. Just talk to him.

MOTEL

Tzeitel, if your father says no, that's it, it's final. He'll yell
at me.

TZEITEL

Motel!

27

MOTEL

I'm just a poor tailor.

TZEITEL

Motel, even a poor tailor is entitled to some happiness.

MOTEL

That's true.

TZEITEL

(*Urgently*)

Will you talk to him? Will you talk to him?

MOTEL

All right, I'll talk to him.

TEVYE

(*Entering*)

It's late! Where is everybody? Late.

MOTEL

(*Following him*)

Reb Tevye —

TEVYE

(*Disregarding him*)

Come in, children, we're lighting the candles.

MOTEL

Reb Tevye. (*Summoning courage*) Reb Tevye, Reb Tevye.

TEVYE

Yes? What is it? (*Loudly*) Well, Motel, what is it?

MOTEL

(*Taken aback*)

Good Sabbath, Reb Tevye.

TEVYE

(*Irritated with him*)

Good Sabbath, Good Sabbath. Come, children, come.

(TEVYE's *family*, PERCHIK, *and* MOTEL *gather around the table.* GOLDE *lights the candles and says a prayer under her breath.*)

28

TEVYE *and* GOLDE
(*Sing to* DAUGHTERS.)

["Sabbath Prayer"]

May the Lord protect and defend you,
May He always shield you from shame,
May you come to be
In Yisroel a shining name.
May you be like Ruth and like Esther,
May you be deserving of praise.
Strengthen them, O Lord,
And keep them from the stranger's ways.

May God bless you
And grant you long lives.

(*The lights go up behind them, showing
other families, behind a transparent curtain,
singing over Sabbath candles.*)

GOLDE
May the Lord fulfill our Sabbath prayer for you.

TEVYE *and* GOLDE
May God make you
Good mothers and wives.

TEVYE
May He send you husbands who will care for you.
TEVYE *and* GOLDE
May the Lord protect and defend you
May the Lord preserve you from pain.
Favor them, O Lord,
With happiness and peace.
O hear our Sabbath prayer.
Amen.

SCENE FOUR

The Inn, the following evening. AVRAM, LAZAR, MENDEL, *and several other people are sitting at tables.* LAZAR *is waiting impatiently, drumming on the tabletop, watching the door.*

LAZAR

Reb Mordcha.

MORDCHA

Yes, Lazar Wolf.

LAZAR

Please bring me a bottle of your best brandy and two glasses.

AVRAM

"Your best brandy," Reb Lazar?

MORDCHA

What's the occasion? Are you getting ready for a party?

LAZAR

There might be a party. Maybe even a wedding.

MORDCHA

A wedding? Wonderful. And I'll be happy to make the wedding merry, lead the dancing, and so forth. For a little fee, naturally.

LAZAR

Naturally, a wedding is no wedding without you — and your fee.

(FYEDKA *enters with several other* RUSSIANS.)

FIRST RUSSIAN

Good evening, Innkeeper.

MORDCHA

Good evening.

FIRST RUSSIAN

We'd like a drink. Sit down, Fyedka.

MORDCHA

Vodka? Schnapps?

Vodka.

MORDCHA

Right away.

> (TEVYE *enters.* LAZAR, *who has been watching the door, turns away, pretending not to be concerned.*)

TEVYE

Good evening.

MORDCHA

Good evening, Tevye.

MENDEL

What are you doing here so early?

TEVYE

(Aside to Mendel)

He wants to buy my new milk cow. Good evening, Reb Lazar.

LAZAR

Ah, Tevye. Sit down. Have a drink. *(Pours a drink.)*

TEVYE

I won't insult you by saying no. *(Drinks.)*

LAZAR

How goes it with you, Tevye?

TEVYE

How should it go?

LAZAR

You're right.

TEVYE

And you?

LAZAR

The same.

TEVYE

I'm sorry to hear that.

31

LAZAR

(*Pours a drink.*)

So how's your brother-in-law in America?

TEVYE

I believe he is doing very well.

LAZAR

He wrote you?

TEVYE

Not lately.

LAZAR

Then how do you know?

TEVYE

If he was doing badly, he would write. May I? (*Pours himself another drink.*)

LAZAR

Tevye, I suppose you know why I wanted to see you.

TEVYE

(*Drinks.*)

Yes, I do, Reb Lazar, but there is no use talking about it.

LAZAR

(*Upset*)

Why not?

TEVYE

Why yes? Why should I get rid of her?

LAZAR

Well, you have a few more without her.

TEVYE

I see! Today you want one. Tomorrow you may want two.

LAZAR

(*Startled*)

Two? What would I do with two?

TEVYE

The same as you do with one!

LAZAR

(*Shocked*)

Tevye! This is very important to me.

TEVYE

Why is it so important to you?

LAZAR

Frankly, because I am lonesome.

TEVYE

(*Startled*)

Lonesome? What are you talking about?

LAZAR

You don't know?

TEVYE

We're talking about my new cow. The one you want to buy
from me.

LAZAR

(*Stares at* TEVYE, *then bursts into laughter.*)

A milk cow! So I won't be lonesome! (*He howls with laughter.*
TEVYE *stares at him.*)

TEVYE

What's so funny?

LAZAR

I was talking about your daughter. Your daughter, Tzeitel!
(*Bursts into laughter.* TEVYE *stares at him, upset.*)

TEVYE

My daughter, Tzeitel?

LAZAR

Of course, your daughter, Tzeitel! I see her in my butcher shop
every Thursday. She's made a good impression on me. I like
her. And as for me, Tevye, as you know, I'm pretty well off.
I have my own house, a good store, a servant. Look, Tevye,
why do we have to try to impress each other? Let's shake hands

33

and call it a match. And you won't need a dowry for her. And maybe you'll find something in your own purse, too.

TEVYE
(*Shouting*)

Shame on you! Shame! (*Hiccups.*) What do you mean, my purse? My Tzeitel is not the sort that I would sell for money!

LAZAR
(*Calming him*)

All right! Just as you say. We won't talk about money. The main thing is, let's get it done with. And I will be good to her, Tevye. (*Slightly embarrassed*) I like her. What do you think?

TEVYE
(*To the audience*)

What do I think? What do I think? I never liked him! Why should I? You can have a fine conversation with him, if you talk about kidneys and livers. On the other hand, not everybody has to be a scholar. If you're wealthy enough, no one will call you stupid. And with a butcher, my daughter will surely never know hunger. Of course, he has a problem — he's much older than her. That's her problem. But she's younger. That's his problem. I always thought of him as a butcher, but I misjudged him. He is a good man. He likes her. He will try to make her happy. (*Turns to* LAZAR.) What do I think? It's a match!

LAZAR
(*Delighted*)

You agree?

TEVYE

I agree.

LAZAR

Oh, Tevye, that's wonderful. Let's drink on it.

TEVYE

Why not? To you.

LAZAR

No, my friend, to you.

TEVYE

To the both of us.

LAZAR

To our agreement.

TEVYE

To our agreement. To our prosperity. To good health and happiness. (*Enter* FIDDLER.) And, most important *(sings),*

["To Life"]

To Life, to Life, L'Chaim.

TEVYE *and* **LAZAR**
L'Chaim, L'Chaim, To Life.

TEVYE
Here's to the father I've tried to be.

LAZAR
Here's to my bride to be.

TEVYE *and* **LAZAR**
Drink, L'Chaim,
To Life, to Life, L'Chaim.
L'Chaim, L'Chaim, to Life.

TEVYE
Life has a way of confusing us,

LAZAR
Blessing and bruising us,
TEVYE *and* **LAZAR**
Drink, L'Chaim, to Life.

TEVYE
God would like us to be joyful,
Even when our hearts lie panting on the floor.

LAZAR

How much more can we be joyful
When there's really something
To be joyful for!

TEVYE *and* LAZAR

To Life, to Life, L'Chaim.

TEVYE

To Tzeitel, my daughter.

LAZAR

My wife.
It gives you something to think about,

TEVYE

Something to drink about,

TEVYE *and* LAZAR

Drink, L'Chaim, to Life.

LAZAR

Reb Mordcha.

MORDCHA

Yes, Lazar Wolf.

LAZAR

Drinks for everybody.

MENDEL

What's the occasion?

LAZAR

I'm taking myself a bride.

VILLAGERS

Who? Who?

LAZAR

Tevye's eldest, Tzeitel.

VILLAGERS

Mazeltov. . . . Wonderful. . . . Congratulations. . . . (*Sing.*)

To Lazar Wolf.

TEVYE

To Tevye.

VILLAGERS

To Tzeitel, your daughter.

LAZAR

My wife.

ALL

May all your futures be pleasant ones,
Not like our present ones.
Drink, L'Chaim, to Life,
To Life, L'Chaim,
L'Chaim, L'Chaim, to Life.
It takes a wedding to make us say,
"Let's live another day,"
Drink, L'Chaim, to Life.

We'll raise a glass and sip a drop of schnapps
In honor of the great good luck
That favored you.

We know that
When good fortune favors two such men
It stands to reason we deserve it, too.
To us and our good fortune.
Be happy, be healthy, long life!
And if our good fortune never comes,
Here's to whatever comes.
Drink, L'Chaim, to Life.

Dai-dai-dai-dai-dai-dai-dai.

(*They begin to dance. A* RUSSIAN *starts to sing, and they stop, uncomfortable.*)

RUSSIAN

Za va sha, Zdarovia,
Heaven bless you both, Nazdrovia,

To your health, and may we live together in peace.

Za va sha, Zdarovia,
Heaven bless you both, Nazdrovia,
To your health, and may we live together in peace.

OTHER RUSSIANS

May you both be favored with the future of your choice.
May you live to see a thousand reasons to rejoice.

Za va sha, Zdarovia,
Heaven bless you both, Nazdrovia,
To your health, and may we live together in peace.
Hey!

(*The* RUSSIANS *begin to dance, the* OTHERS *join in and they dance to a wild finale pileup on the bar.*)

TEVYE
(*From the pileup*)
To Life!

(*Blackout*)

SCENE FIVE

The street outside the Inn. Entering through the inn door are the FIDDLER, LAZAR, TEVYE, *the other* VILLAGERS, *and the* RUSSIANS, *singing "To Life."*

LAZAR

You know, Tevye, after the marriage, we will be related. You will be my papa.

TEVYE

Your papa! I always wanted a son, but I wanted one a little younger than myself.

(The CONSTABLE *enters.)*

CONSTABLE

Good evening.

FIRST RUSSIAN

Good evening, Constable.

CONSTABLE

What's the celebration?

FIRST RUSSIAN

Tevye is marrying off his oldest daughter.

CONSTABLE

May I offer my congratulations, Tevye?

TEVYE

Thank you, your Honor.

(All but TEVYE *and the* CONSTABLE *exit.)*

CONSTABLE

Oh, Tevye, I have a piece of news that I think I should tell you, as a friend.

TEVYE

Yes, your Honor?

CONSTABLE

And I'm giving you this news because I like you. You are a decent, honest person, even though you are a Jewish dog.

TEVYE

How often does a man get a compliment like that? And your news?

CONSTABLE

We have received orders that sometime soon this district is to have a little unofficial demonstration.

TEVYE
(Shocked)

A pogrom? Here?

39

CONSTABLE

No — just a little unofficial demonstration.

TEVYE

How little?

CONSTABLE

Not too serious — just some mischief, so that if an inspector comes through, he will see that we have done our duty. Personally, I don't know why there has to be this trouble between people, but I thought I should tell you, and you can tell the others.

TEVYE

Thank you, your Honor. You're a good man. If I may say so, it's too bad you're not a Jew.

CONSTABLE

(Amused)

That's what I like about you, Tevye, always joking. And congratulations again, for your daughter.

TEVYE

Thank you, your Honor. Goodbye. (The CONSTABLE exits. TEVYE turns to heaven.) Dear God, did You have to send me news like that, today of all days? It's true that we are the Chosen People. But once in a while can't You choose someone else? Anyway, thank You for sending a husband for my Tzeitel. L'Chaim.

(The FIDDLER enters, he circles TEVYE, and they dance off together.)

SCENE SIX

Outside TEVYE's *house.* PERCHIK *is teaching* SHPRINTZE *and* BIELKE *while they peel potatoes at a bench.* HODEL *is cleaning pails at the pump.*

40

Now, children, I will tell you the story from the Bible, of Laban and Jacob, and then we will discuss it together. All right? *(They nod.)* Good. Now Laban had two daughters, Leah and the beautiful Rachel. And Jacob loved the younger, Rachel, and he asked Laban for her hand. Laban agreed, if Jacob would work for him for seven years.

SHPRINTZE

Was Laban a mean man?

PERCHIK

(Dryly)

He was an employer! Now, after Jacob worked seven years, do you know what happened? Laban fooled him, and gave him his ugly daughter, Leah. So, to marry Rachel, Jacob was forced to work another seven years. You see, children, the Bible clearly teaches us, you must never trust an employer. Do you understand?

SHPRINTZE

Yes, Perchik.

BIELKE

Yes, Perchik.

PERCHIK

Good, now —

GOLDE

(Entering from the barn)

Papa isn't up yet?

HODEL

No, Mama.

GOLDE

Then enough lessons. We have to do Papa's work today. How long can he sleep? He staggered home last night and fell into bed like a dead man. I couldn't get a word out of him. **Put**

41

that away and clean the barn. (SHPRINTZE *and* BIELKE *exit into the barn. To* HODEL) Call me when Papa gets up. (GOLDE *exits.* HODEL *pumps a bucket of water.*)

HODEL

That was a very interesting lesson, Perchik.

PERCHIK

Do you think so?

HODEL

Although I don't know if the rabbi would agree with your interpretation.

PERCHIK

And neither, I suppose, would the rabbi's son.

HODEL

My little sisters have big tongues.

PERCHIK

And what do you know about him, except that he is the rabbi's son? Would you be interested in him if he were the shoe-maker's son, or the tinsmith's son?

HODEL

At least I know this, he does not have any strange ideas about turning the world upside down.

PERCHIK

Certainly. Any new idea would be strange to you. Remember, the Lord said, "Let there be light."

HODEL

Yes, but He was not talking to you personally. Good day. (*Starts off.*)

PERCHIK

You have spirit. Even a little intelligence, perhaps.

HODEL

Thank you.

PERCHIK

But what good is your brain? Without curiosity it is a rusty tool. Good day, Hodel.

HODEL

We have an old custom here. A boy acts respectfully to a girl. But, of course, that is too traditional for an advanced thinker like you.

PERCHIK

Our traditions! Nothing must change! Everything is perfect exactly the way it is!

HODEL

We like our ways.

PERCHIK

Our ways are changing all over but here. Here men and women must keep apart. Men study. Women in the kitchen. Boys and girls must not touch, should not even look at each other.

HODEL

I am looking at you!

PERCHIK

You are very brave! Do you know that in the city boys and girls can be affectionate without permission of a matchmaker? They hold hands together, they even dance together — new dances — like this. (*He seizes her and starts dancing, humming.*) I learned it in Kiev. Do you like it?

HODEL

(*Startled*)

It's very nice.

PERCHIK

(*Stops dancing.*)

There. We've just changed an old custom.

HODEL

(*Bewildered*)

Yes. Well, you're welcome — I mean, thank you — I mean, good day.

43

PERCHIK
Good day!

(TEVYE *enters, suffering from a headache.*)

TEVYE

Bielke, Shprintze, what's your name?

HODEL

Hodel, Papa.

TEVYE

Where is Tzeitel?

HODEL

She's in the barn.

TEVYE

Call her out. (HODEL *exits into the barn.*) Reb Perchik. How did the lesson go today?

PERCHIK

(*Watching* HODEL's *exit*)

I think we made a good beginning.

(*Enter* GOLDE.)

GOLDE

Ah, he's finally up. What happened last night, besides your drinking like a peasant? Did you see Lazar Wolf? What did he say? What did you say? Do you have news?

TEVYE

Patience, woman. As the Good Book says, "Good news will stay and bad news will refuse to leave." And there's another saying that goes —

GOLDE

(*Exasperated*)

You can die from such a man!

(TZEITEL *enters from the barn.* HODEL *and* CHAVA *follow her.*)

44

TEVYE

Ah, Tzeitel, my lamb, come here. Tzeitel, you are to be congratulated. You are going to be married!

GOLDE

Married!

TZEITEL

What do you mean, Papa?

TEVYE

Lazar Wolf has asked for your hand.

GOLDE
(Thrilled)

I knew it!

TZEITEL
(Bewildered)

The butcher?

GOLDE
(Enraptured)

My heart told me this was our lucky day. O dear God, I thank Thee, I thank Thee.

TEVYE

And what do you say, Tzeitel?

GOLDE

What can she say? My first-born, a bride! May you grow old with him in fortune and honor, not like Fruma-Sarah, that first wife of his. She was a bitter woman, may she rest in peace. Not like my Tzeitel. And now I must thank Yente. My Tzeitel, a bride! *(She hurries off.)*

HODEL *and* **CHAVA**
(Subdued)

Mazeltov, Tzeitel.

TEVYE

You call that a Mazeltov? (**HODEL** *and* **CHAVA** *exit.*) And you, Reb Perchik, aren't you going to congratulate her?

45

PERCHIK

(*Sarcastic*)

Congratulations, Tzeitel, for getting a rich man.

TEVYE

Again with the rich! What's wrong with being rich?

PERCHIK

It is no reason to marry. Money is the world's curse.

TEVYE

May the Lord smite me with it! And may I never recover! Tzeitel knows I mean only her welfare. Am I right, Tzeitel?

TZEITEL

Yes, Papa.

TEVYE

You see.

PERCHIK

I see. I see very well. (*He exits.*)

TEVYE

Well, Tzeitel, my child, why are you so silent? Aren't you happy with this blessing?

TZEITEL

(*Bursts into tears.*)

Oh, Papa, Papa.

TEVYE

What is it? Tell me.

TZEITEL

Papa, I don't want to marry him. I can't marry him. I can't —

TEVYE

What do you mean, you can't? If I say you will, you will.

TZEITEL

Papa, if it's a matter of money, I'll do anything. I'll hire my-self out as a servant. I'll dig ditches, I'll haul rocks, only don't make me marry him, Papa, please.

46

TEVYE

What's wrong with Lazar? He likes you.

TZEITEL

Papa, I will be unhappy with him. All my life will be unhappy. I'll dig ditches, I'll haul rocks.

TEVYE

But we made an agreement. With us an agreement is an agreement.

TZEITEL

(Simply)

Is that more important than I am, Papa? Papa, don't force me. I'll be unhappy all my days.

TEVYE

All right. I won't force you.

TZEITEL

Oh, thank you, Papa.

TEVYE

It seems it was not ordained that you should have all the comforts of life, or that we should have a little joy in our old age after all our hard work.

(Enter MOTEL, *breathless.)*

MOTEL

Reb Tevye, may I speak to you?

TEVYE

Later, Motel. Later.

MOTEL

I would like to speak to you.

TEVYE

Not now, Motel. I have problems.

MOTEL

That's what I want to speak to you about. I think I can help.

TEVYE

Certainly. Like a bandage can help a corpse. Goodbye, Motel.
Goodbye.

TZEITEL

At least listen to him, Papa.

TEVYE

All right. You have a tongue, talk.

MOTEL

Reb Tevye, I hear you are arranging a match for Tzeitel.

TEVYE

He also has ears.

MOTEL

I have a match for Tzeitel.

TEVYE

What kind of match?

MOTEL

A perfect fit.

TEVYE

A perfect fit.

MOTEL

Like a glove.

TEVYE

Like a glove.

MOTEL

This match was made exactly to measure.

TEVYE

A perfect fit. Made to measure. Stop talking like a tailor and
tell me who it is.

MOTEL

Please, don't shout at me.

TEVYE

All right. Who is it?

MOTEL

Who is it?

TEVYE

(*Pauses*)

Who is it?

MOTEL

Who is it?

TEVYE

Who is it?

MOTEL

It's me — myself.

TEVYE

(*Stares at him, then turns to the audience,
startled and amused.*)

Him? Himself? (*To* MOTEL) Either you're completely out of
your mind or you're crazy. (*To the audience*) He must be
crazy. (*To* MOTEL) Arranging a match for yourself. What are
you, everything? The bridegroom, the matchmaker, the guests
all rolled into one? I suppose you'll even perform the cere-
mony. You must be crazy!

MOTEL

Please don't shout at me, Reb Tevye. As for being my own
matchmaker, I know it's a little unusual.

TEVYE

Unusual? It's crazy.

MOTEL

Times are changing, Reb Tevye. The thing is, your daughter
Tzeitel and I gave each other our pledge more than a year ago
that we would marry.

TEVYE

(*Stunned*)

You gave each other your pledge?

49

TZEITEL

Yes, Papa, we gave each other our pledge.

TEVYE

(Looks at them, turns to the audience. Sings.)

["Tradition" Reprise]

They gave each other a pledge.
Unheard of, absurd.
You gave each other a pledge?
Unthinkable.
Where do you think you are?
In Moscow?
In Paris?
Where do they think they are?
America?
What do you think you're doing?
You stitcher, you nothing!
Who do you think you are?
King Solomon?
This isn't the way it's done,
Not here, not now.
Some things I will not, I cannot, allow.
Tradition —
Marriages must be arranged by the papa.
This should never be changed.
One little time you pull out a prop,
And where does it stop?
Where does it stop?

(Speaks.)

Where does it stop? Do I still have something to say about my daughter, or doesn't anyone have to ask a father any more?

50

MOTEL

I have wanted to ask you for some time, Reb Tevye, but first I wanted to save up for my own sewing machine.

TEVYE

Stop talking nonsense. You're just a poor tailor.

MOTEL
(*Bravely*)

That's true, Reb Tevye, but even a poor tailor is entitled to some happiness. (*Looks at* TZEITEL *triumphantly.*) I promise you, Reb Tevye, your daughter will not starve.

TEVYE
(*Impressed, turns to the audience.*)

He's beginning to talk like a man. On the other hand, what kind of match would that be, with a poor tailor? On the other hand, he's an honest, hard worker. On the other hand, he has absolutely nothing. On the other hand, things could never get worse for him, they could only get better. (*Sings.*)

> They gave each other a pledge —
> Unheard of, absurd.
> They gave each other a pledge —
> Unthinkable.
> But look at my daughter's face —
> She loves him, she wants him —
> And look at my daughter's eyes,
> So hopeful.
>
> (*Shrugs. To the audience*)
> Tradition!

(*To* TZEITEL *and* MOTEL)
Well, children, when shall we make the wedding?

TZEITEL

Thank you, Papa.

MOTEL

Reb Tevye, you won't be sorry.

TEVYE

I won't be sorry? I'm sorry already!

TZEITEL

Thank you, Papa.

MOTEL

Thank you, Papa.

TEVYE

Thank you, Papa! They pledged their troth! (*Starts to exit, then looks back at them.*) Modern children! (*Has a sudden thought.*) Golde! What will I tell Golde? What am I going to do about Golde? (*To heaven.*) Help! (*Exits.*)

TZEITEL

Motel, you were wonderful!

MOTEL

It was a miracle! It was a miracle. (*Sings.*)

["Miracle of Miracles"]

Wonder of wonders, miracle of miracles,
God took a Daniel once again,
Stood by his side, and miracle of miracles,
Walked him through the lion's den.

Wonder of wonders, miracle of miracles,
I was afraid that God would frown.
But, like He did so long ago in Jericho,
God just made a wall fall down.

When Moses softened Pharoah's heart,
That was a miracle.
When God made the waters of the Red Sea part,
That was a miracle, too.

But of all God's miracles large and small,

52

The most miraculous one of all
Is that out of a worthless lump of clay
God has made a man today.

Wonder of wonders, miracle of miracles,
God took a tailor by the hand,
Turned him around, and, miracle of miracles,
Led him to the Promised Land.

When David slew Goliath, yes!
That was a miracle.
When God gave us manna in the wilderness,
That was a miracle, too.

But of all God's miracles, large and small,
The most miraculous one of all
Is the one I thought could never be —
God has given you to me.

SCENE SEVEN

TEVYE's *bedroom. The room is in complete darkness. A groan is heard, then another, then a scream.*

TEVYE

Aagh! Lazar! Motel! Tzeitel!

GOLDE

What is it? What?

TEVYE

Help! Help! Help!

GOLDE

Tevye, wake up! (GOLDE *lights the lamp. The light reveals* TEVYE *asleep in bed.*)

TEVYE

(In his sleep)

Help! Help!

53

GOLDE

(*Shaking him*)

Tevye! What's the matter with you? Why are you howling like that?

TEVYE

(*Opening his eyes, frightened*)

Where is she? Where is she?

GOLDE

Where is who? What are you talking about?

TEVYE

Fruma-Sarah. Lazar Wolf's first wife, Fruma-Sarah. She was standing here a minute ago.

GOLDE

What's the matter with you, Tevye? Fruma-Sarah has been dead for years. You must have been dreaming. Tell me what you dreamt, and I'll tell you what it meant.

TEVYE

It was terrible.

GOLDE

Tell me.

TEVYE

All right — only don't be frightened!

GOLDE

(*Impatiently*)

Tell me!

TEVYE

All right, this was my dream. In the beginning I dreamt that we were having a celebration of some kind. Everybody we knew was there, and musicians too.

(*As he speaks,* MEN, *including a* RABBI, WOMEN *and* MUSICIANS *enter the bedroom.* TEVYE, *wearing a nightshirt, starts to get out of bed to join the dream.*)

54

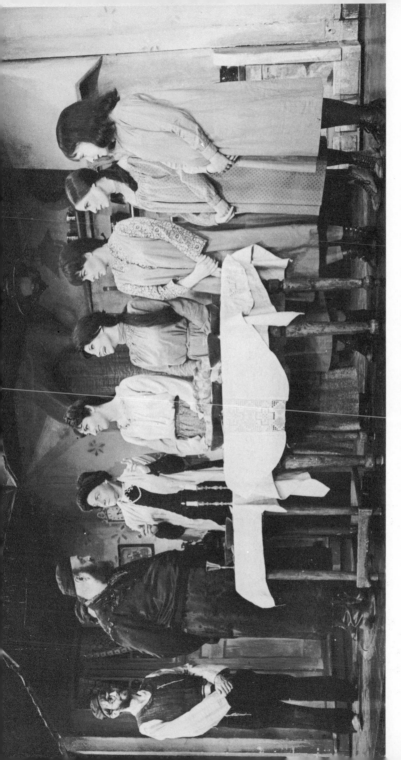

Austin Pendleton, Bert Convy, Zero Mostel, Maria Karnilova, Joanna Merlin, Julia Migenes, Tanya Everett, Marilyn Rogers, and Linda Ross—lighting the Sabbath candles

Zero Mostel, Michael Granger, and villagers—"To Life"

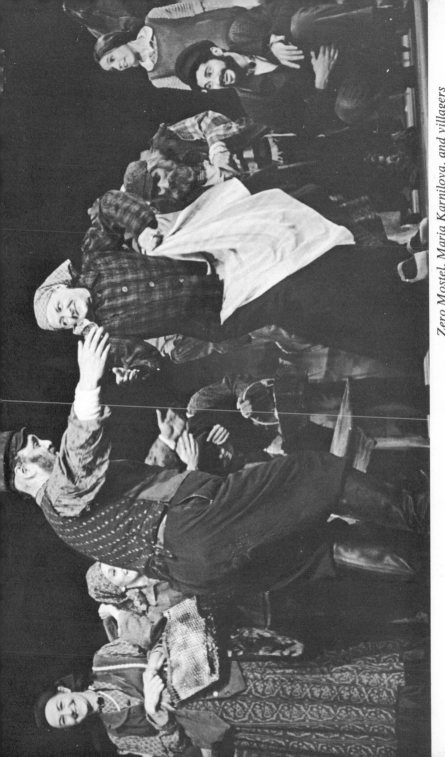

Zero Mostel, Maria Karnilova, and villagers

Maria Karnilova, Zero Mostel, Sue Babel, and villagers—dream about Grandma Tzeitel

In the middle of the dream, in walks your Grandmother Tzeitel, may she rest in peace.

GOLDE
(*Alarmed*)
Grandmother Tzeitel? How did she look?

TEVYE
For a woman who is dead thirty years, she looked very good. Naturally, I went up to greet her. She said to me —

(GRANDMA TZEITEL *enters, and* TEVYE *approaches her and greets her in pantomime.* GRANDMA *sings.*)

["The Tailor, Motel Kamzoil"]

GRANDMA TZEITEL
A blessing on your head,

RABBI
Mazeltov, Mazeltov.

GRANDMA TZEITEL
To see a daughter wed.

RABBI
Mazeltov, Mazeltov.

GRANDMA TZEITEL
And such a son-in-law,
Like no one ever saw,
The tailor Motel Kamzoil.

GOLDE
(*Bewildered*)

Motel?

GRANDMA TZEITEL
A worthy boy is he,

RABBI
Mazeltov, Mazeltov.

55

GRANDMA TZEITEL

Of pious family.

RABBI

Mazeltov, Mazeltov.

GRANDMA TZEITEL

They named him after my
Dear Uncle Mordecai,
The tailor Motel Kamzoil.

GOLDE

A tailor! She must have heard wrong. She meant a butcher.

(TEVYE, *who has returned to* GOLDE,
listens to this, then runs back to
GRANDMA TZEITEL.)

TEVYE

You must have heard wrong, Grandma,
There's no tailor,
You mean a butcher, Grandma,
By the name of Lazar Wolf.

GRANDMA TZEITEL

(*Flies into the air, screaming angrily*)

No!!

(*Sings.*)
I mean a tailor, Tevye.
My great grandchild,
My little Tzeitel, who you named for me,
Motel's bride was meant to be.
For such a match I prayed.

CHORUS

Mazeltov, Mazeltov,

GRANDMA TZEITEL

In heaven it was made.

Mazeltov, Mazeltov,

GRANDMA TZEITEL

A fine upstanding boy,
A comfort and a joy,
The tailor Motel Kamzoil.

GOLDE

(From bed)

But we announced it already. We made a bargain with the butcher.

TEVYE

But we announced it, Grandma,
To our neighbors.
We made a bargain, Grandma,
With the butcher, Lazar Wolf.

GRANDMA TZEITEL

(Again flies into the air, screaming angrily)

No!!

(Sings.)

So you announced it, Tevye,
That's your headache.
But as for Lazar Wolf, I say to you,
Tevye, that's your headache, too.

CHORUS

A blessing on your house, Mazeltov, Mazeltov,
Imagine such a spouse, Mazeltov, Mazeltov,
And such a son-in-law,
Like no one ever saw,
The tailor Motel Kamzoil.

(Speaks.)

It was a butcher!

CHORUS

The tailor Motel Kamzoil.

TEVYE

(Speaks.)

It was Lazar Wolfe!

(Sings.)

The tailor Motel Kam . . .

CHORUS

Shah! shah!

Look!

Who is this?

Who is this?

Who comes here?

Who? who? who? who? who?

What woman is this

By righteous anger shaken?

SOLO VOICES

Could it be?

Sure!

Yes, it could!

Why not?

Who could be mistaken?

CHORUS

It's the butcher's wife come from beyond the grave.

It's the butcher's dear, darling, departed wife,

Fruma-Sarah, Fruma-Sarah

Fruma-Sarah, Fruma-Sarah, Fruma-Sarah.

FRUMA-SARAH

Tevye! Tevye!

What is this about your daughter marrying my husband?

58

CHORUS

Yes, her husband.

FRUMA-SARAH

Would you do this to your friend and neighbor,
Fruma-Sarah?

CHORUS

Fruma-Sarah.

FRUMA-SARAH

Have you no consideration for a woman's feelings?

CHORUS

Woman's feelings.

FRUMA-SARAH

Handing over my belongings to a total stranger.

CHORUS

Total stranger.

FRUMA-SARAH

How can you allow it, how?
How can you let your daughter take my place?
Live in my house, carry my keys,
And wear my clothes, pearls — how?

CHORUS

How can you allow your daughter
To take her place?

FRUMA-SARAH

Pearls!

CHORUS

House!

FRUMA-SARAH

Pearls!

CHORUS

Keys!

FRUMA-SARAH

Pearls!

CHORUS

Clothes!

FRUMA-SARAH

Pearls!

CHORUS

How?

FRUMA-SARAH

Tevye!!

CHORUS

Tevye!!

FRUMA-SARAH

Such a learned man as Tevye wouldn't let it happen.

CHORUS

Let it happen.

FRUMA-SARAH

Tell me that it isn't true, and then I wouldn't worry.

CHORUS

Wouldn't worry.

FRUMA-SARAH

Say you didn't give your blessing to your daughter's
Marriage.

CHORUS

Daughter's marriage.

FRUMA-SARAH

Let me tell you what would follow such a fatal wedding.

CHORUS

Fatal wedding.
Shh!

FRUMA-SARAH

If Tzeitel marries Lazar Wolf,
I pity them both.
She'll live with him three weeks,

And when three weeks are up,
I'll come to her by night,
I'll take her by the throat, and . . .
This I'll give your Tzeitel,
That I'll give your Tzeitel,
This I'll give your Tzeitel,
(*Laughs wildly.*)
Here's my wedding present if she marries Lazar Wolfe!

(*She starts choking Tevye. The* CHORUS *exits screaming.*)

GOLDE

(*While* TEVYE *is being choked*)
It's an evil spirit; May it fall into the river; may it sink into the
earth. Such a dark and horrible dream! And to think it was
brought on by that butcher. If my Grandmother Tzeitel, may
she rest in peace, took the trouble to come all the way from
the other world to tell us about the tailor, all we can say is that
it is all for the best, and it couldn't possibly be any better. Amen.

TEVYE

Amen.

GOLDE

(*Sings.*)
A blessing on my head, Mazeltov, Mazeltov,
Like Grandma Tzeitel said, Mazeltov, Mazeltov.
We'll have a son-in-law,
Like no one ever saw,
The tailor Motel Kamzoil.

TEVYE

We haven't got the man,

GOLDE

Mazeltov, Mazeltov.

TEVYE

We had when we began.

61

GOLDE

Mazeltov, Mazeltov.

TEVYE

But since your Grandma came,
She'll marry what's his name?

GOLDE

The tailor Motel Kamzoil.

TEVYE *and* GOLDE

The tailor Motel Kamzoil,
The tailor Motel Kamzoil,
The tailor Motel Kamzoil.

(GOLDE *goes back to sleep.* TEVYE *mouths the
words "Thank You" to God, and goes to sleep.*)

SCENE EIGHT

The village street and the interior of MOTEL'*s tailor shop.*
MOTEL *and* CHAVA *are in the shop.* VILLAGERS *pass by.*

MAN

Bagels, fresh bagels.

WOMAN
(Excited)

Did you hear? Did you hear? Tevye's Tzeitel is marrying
Motel, not Lazar Wolf.

VILLAGERS

No!

WOMAN

Yes.

MENDEL

Tzeitel is marrying Motel?

WOMAN

Yes!

62

No! (*They rush into the shop and surround* MOTEL. MORDCHA *enters the street.*) Mazeltov, Motel. Congratulations.

MORDCHA

What's all the excitement?

AVRAM

Tevye's Tzeitel is going to marry —

MORDCHA

I know. Lazar Wolf, the butcher. It's wonderful.

AVRAM

No. Motel, the tailor.

MORDCHA

Motel, the tailor, that's terrible! (*Rushes into the shop.*) Mazeltov, Motel.

WOMAN

(*To* SHANDEL, *exiting from the shop*)

Imagine! Tzeitel is marrying Motel. I can't believe it!

SHANDEL

(*Outraged*)

What's wrong with my son, Motel?

WOMAN

Oh, excuse me, Shandel. Mazeltov.

VILLAGERS

(*Inside the shop*)

Mazeltov, Mazeltov.

MOTEL

Yussel, do you have a wedding hat for me?

YUSSEL

Lazar Wolf ordered a hat but it's not cheap.

MOTEL

I got his bride, I can get his hat!

YUSSEL

Then come, Motel, come.

Chava, can you watch the shop for a few minutes? I'll be back soon.

CHAVA

Of course.

MOTEL

Thank you, Chava. *(They all exit from the shop, calling Mazeltovs.)*

VILLAGERS
(To CHAVA)

We just heard about your sister. . . . Mazeltov, Chava. . . . Mazeltov, Chava.

CHAVA

Thanks — thank you very much.

(All but CHAVA exit. FYEDKA, SASHA and another RUSSIAN enter at the same time. They cross to CHAVA, blocking her way into the shop.)

SASHA *and* RUSSIAN

(Mockingly, imitating others, with a slight mispronunciation)
Mazeltov, Chava. Mazeltov, Chava.

CHAVA

Please may I pass.

SASHA
(Getting in her way)

Why? We're congratulating you.

RUSSIAN

Mazeltov, Chava.

FYEDKA
(Calmly)

All right, stop it.

SASHA

What's wrong with you?

FYEDKA

Just stop it.

64

SASHA

Now listen here, Fyedka —

FYEDKA

Goodbye, Sasha. (SASHA *and the* RUSSIAN *hesitate.*) I said goodbye! (*They look at* FYEDKA *curiously, then exit.*) I'm sorry
about that. They mean no harm.

CHAVA

Don't they? (*She enters shop. He follows her.*) Is there something you want?

FYEDKA

Yes. I'd like to talk to you.

CHAVA

I'd rather not. (*She hesitates.*)

FYEDKA

I've often noticed you at the bookseller's. Not many girls in
this village like to read. (*A sudden thought strikes him. He ex-
tends the book he is holding.*) Would you like to borrow this
book? It's very good.

CHAVA

No, thank you.

FYEDKA

Why? Because I'm not Jewish? Do you feel about us the way
they feel about you? I didn't think you would. And what do
you know about me? Let me tell you about myself. I'm a
pleasant fellow, charming, honest, ambitious, quite bright, and
very modest.

CHAVA

I don't think we should be talking this way.

FYEDKA

I often do things I shouldn't. Go ahead, take the book. It's by
Heinrich Heine. Happens to be Jewish, I believe.

CHAVA

That doesn't matter.

65

FYEDKA

You're quite right. *(She takes the book.)* Good. After you return it, I'll ask you how you like it, and we'll talk about it for a while. Then we'll talk about life, how we feel about things, and it can all turn out quite pleasant.

(CHAVA *puts the book on the table as* MOTEL *enters.*)

MOTEL

Oh, Fyedka! Can I do something for you?

FYEDKA

No, thank you. *(Starts to leave.)*

MOTEL

Oh. you forgot your book.

CHAVA

No, it's mine.

MOTEL

Thank you, Chava. (CHAVA *takes the book and leaves the shop with* FYEDKA.)

FYEDKA
(Outside)

Good day, Chava.

CHAVA

Good day.

FYEDKA
(Pleasantly)

Fyedka.

CHAVA

Good day, Fyedka. *(They exit.* MOTEL *puts on his wedding hat.)*

SCENE NINE

Part of TEVYE's *yard. Night.* TZEITEL, *in a bridal gown, enters, followed by* TEVYE, GOLDE, HODEL, BIELKE, CHAVA, SHPRINTZE, *and* RELATIONS. MOTEL *enters, followed by his*

PARENTS *and* RELATIONS. *Many* GUESTS *enter, carrying lit candles. The men take their places on the right, as a group, the women on the left;* TZEITEL *and* MOTEL *stand in the center.* MOTEL *places a veil over* TZEITEL's *head.* FOUR MEN *enter, carrying a canopy. They are followed by the* RABBI. *The canopy is placed over* MOTEL *and* TZEITEL. GUESTS *start singing.*

["Sunrise, Sunset"]

TEVYE
Is this the little girl I carried?
Is this the little boy at play?

GOLDE
I don't remember growing older.
When did they?

TEVYE
When did she get to be a beauty?
When did he grow to be so tall?

GOLDE
Wasn't it yesterday when they were small?

MEN
Sunrise, sunset,
Sunrise, sunset,
Swiftly flow the days.
Seedlings turn overnight to sunflowers,
Blossoming even as we gaze.

WOMEN
Sunrise, sunset,
Sunrise, sunset,
Swiftly fly the years.
One season following another,
Laden with happiness and tears.

67

TEVYE
What words of wisdom can I give them?
How can I help to ease their way?
GOLDE
Now they must learn from one another
Day by day.
PERCHIK
They look so natural together.
HODEL
Just like two newlyweds should be.
PERCHIK *and* HODEL
Is there a canopy in store for me?

ALL
Sunrise, sunset,
Sunrise, sunset,
Swiftly fly the years.
One season following another,
Laden with happiness and tears.

(During the song, the following mime is performed. The
RABBI *lifts* TZEITEL's *veil. He prays over a goblet of wine and*
hands it to the bride and groom. They each sip from it. TZEITEL
slowly walks in a circle around MOTEL. MOTEL *places a ring on*
TZEITEL's *finger. The* RABBI *places a wineglass on the floor.*
The song ends. A moment's pause. MOTEL *treads on the glass.)*

ALL
(At the moment the glass breaks)
Mazeltov!

SCENE TEN
The set opens to show the entire yard of TEVYE's *house. Part*
of it is divided down the center by a short partition. Several
tables are set up at the rear of each section. The MUSICIANS

play, and all dance and then seat themselves on benches at the
tables. The women are on the left, the men on the right. As the
dance concludes, MORDCHA *mounts a stool and signals for silence.*
The noise subsides.

ALL

Shah. Shah. Quiet. Reb Mordcha. Shah. Shah.

MORDCHA

My friends, we are gathered here to share the joy of the newlyweds, Motel and Tzeitel. May they live together in peace to a
ripe old age. Amen.

ALL

Amen.

(The RABBI *slowly makes his way to the*
table, assisted by MENDEL.*)*

MORDCHA

Ah, here comes our beloved rabbi. May he be with us for many,
many years.

RABBI
(Ahead of the others)

Amen.

ALL

Amen.

MORDCHA

I want to announce that the bride's parents are giving the newlyweds the following: a new featherbed, a pair of pillows —

GOLDE
(Shouting from the women's side)

Goose pillows.

MORDCHA

Goose pillows. And this pair of candlesticks.

ALL

Mazeltov!

MORDCHA

Now let us not in our joy tonight forget those who are no longer with us, our dear departed, who lived in pain and poverty and hardship and who died in pain and poverty and hardship. (*All sob. He pauses a moment.*) But enough tears. (*The mourning stops immediately.*) Let's be merry and content, like our good friend, Lazar Wolf, who has everything in the world, except a bride. (*Laughter.*) But Lazar has no ill feelings. In fact, he has a gift for the newlyweds that he wants to announce himself. Come, Lazar Wolf.

LAZAR
(*Rising*)

Like he said, I have no ill feelings. What's done is done. I am giving the newlyweds five chickens, one for each of the first five Sabbaths of their wedded life. (*Murmurs of appreciation from all.*)

TEVYE
(*Rising*)

Reb Lazar, you are a decent man. In the name of my daughter and her new husband, I accept your gift. There is a famous saying that —

LAZAR

Reb Tevye, I'm not marrying your daughter. I don't have to listen to your sayings.

TEVYE

If you would listen a second, I was only going to say —

LAZAR

Why should I listen to you? A man who breaks an agreement!

(*Murmurs by the assemblage.*)

MENDEL

Not now, Lazar, in the middle of a wedding.

70

LAZAR

I have a right to talk.

TEVYE

(*Angry*)

What right? This is not your wedding.

LAZAR

It should have been!

(*Murmurs by the assemblage.*)

MENDEL

Reb Lazar, don't shame Reb Tevye at his daughter's wedding.

LAZAR

But he shamed me in front of the whole village!

(*An argument breaks out. Everyone takes sides.*)

ALL

That's true. . . . The rabbi said . . . It was a shame . . . He has
no feelings . . . This is not the place —

MENDEL

Shah. Shah. Quiet. The rabbi. The rabbi, the rabbi.

RABBI

(*Rising, as the noise subsides.*)

I say — Let's sit down. (*Sits.*)

TEVYE

We all heard the wise words of the rabbi.

(*Everyone returns to his seat.*)

MORDCHA

Now, I'd like to sing a little song that —

TEVYE

(*Bursting out*)

You can keep your diseased chickens!

LAZAR

Leave my chickens out of this. We made a bargain.

TEVYE

The terms weren't settled.

LAZAR

We drank on it —

FIRST MAN

I saw them, they drank on it.

SECOND MAN

But the terms weren't settled.

SHANDEL

What's done is done.

TEVYE

Once a butcher, always a butcher.

GOLDE

I had a sign. My own grandmother came to us from the grave.

YENTE

What sign? What grandmother? My grandfather came to me from the grave and told me that her grandmother was a big liar.

LAZAR

We drank on it.

(Bedlam. MORDCHA tries to quiet the guests. PERCHIK climbs onto a stool, hanging two tin plates together.)

MORDCHA

Quiet, I'm singing.

TEVYE

The terms weren't settled.

GOLDE

I had a sign.

YENTE

An agreement is an agreement.

72

PERCHIK

(*Silences them.*)

Quiet! Quiet! What's all the screaming about? "They drank on it — " "An agreement — " "A sign." It's all nonsense. Tzeitel wanted to marry Motel and not Lazar.

MENDEL

A young girl decides for herself?

PERCHIK

Why not? Yes! They love each other.

AVRAM

Love!

LAZAR

Terrible!

MENDEL

He's a radical!

YENTE

What happens to the matchmaker?

(*Another violent argument breaks out.*)

RABBI

I say — I say — (*They all turn to him.*)

TEVYE

Let's sit down? (*Rabbi nods.*)

MORDCHA

Musicians, play. A dance, a dance! (*The music starts, but no one dances.*) Come on, dance. It's a wedding.

YENTE

Some wedding!

(PERCHIK *crosses to the women's side.*)

AVRAM

What's he doing?

TEVYE

Perchik!

FIRST MAN

Stop him!

PERCHIK
(*To* HODEL)

Who will dance with me?

MENDEL

That's a sin!

PERCHIK

It's no sin to dance at a wedding.

AVRAM

But with a girl?

LAZAR

That's what comes from bringing a wild man into your house.

TEVYE
(*Signalling* PERCHIK *to return to the men's side*)

He's not a wild man. His ideas are a little different, but —

MENDEL

It's a sin.

PERCHIK

It's no sin. Ask the rabbi. Ask him. (*They all gather around the* RABBI.)

TEVYE

Well, Rabbi?

RABBI
(*Thumbs through a book, finds the place.*)

Dancing — Well, it's not exactly forbidden, but —

TEVYE

There, you see? It's not forbidden.

PERCHIK
(*To* HODEL)

And it's no sin. Now will someone dance with me? (HODEL *rises to dance.*)

74

GOLDE

Hodel!

HODEL

It's only a dance, Mama.

PERCHIK

Play! (PERCHIK *and* HODEL *dance.*)

LAZAR

Look at Tevye's daughter.

MENDEL

She's dancing with a man.

TEVYE

I can see she's dancing (*Starts toward them as if to stop them. Changes his mind.*) And I'm going to dance with my wife. Golde! (*Golde hesitates, then dances with him.*)

SHANDEL

Golde! (MOTEL *crosses to* TZEITEL.) Motel!

(TZEITEL *dances with* MOTEL. *Others joint them. They all dance, except for* LAZAR *and* YENTE, *who storm off. As the dance reaches a wild climax, the* CONSTABLE *and his* MEN *enter, carrying clubs. The dancers see them and slowly stop.*)

CONSTABLE

I see we came at a bad time, Tevye. I'm sorry, but the orders are for tonight. For the whole village. (*To the* MUSICIANS) Go on, play, play. All right, men.

(*The* RUSSIANS *begin their destruction, turning over tables, throwing pillows, smashing dishes and the window of the house. One of them throws the wedding-gift candlesticks to the ground, and* PER-CHIK *grapples with him. But he is hit*

75

with a club and falls to the ground. The
GUESTS *leave.)*

HODEL
(Rushes to PERCHIK)
No, Perchik!

(The GUESTS *have left during the above action.)*

CONSTABLE
(To his MEN)
All right, enough! *(To* TEVYE) I am genuinely sorry. You understand. (TEVYE *does not answer. To his* MEN) Come. *(The* CONSTABLE *and his* MEN *exit.)*

GOLDE
Take him in the house. (HODEL *helps* PERCHIK *into the house.)*

TEVYE
(Quietly)
What are you standing around for? Clean up. Clean up.

(They start straightening up, picking up broken dishes, bringing bedding back to the house. TZEITEL *picks up candlesticks, one of which is broken. They freeze at sudden sounds of destruction in a nearby house, then continue straightening up as the curtain falls.)*

ACT TWO

PROLOGUE

The exterior of TEVYE's *house.* TEVYE *is sitting on a bench.*

TEVYE
(To heaven)

That was quite a dowry You gave my daughter Tzeitel at her wedding. Was that necessary? Anyway, Tzeitel and Motel have been married almost two months now. They work very hard, they are as poor as squirrels in winter. But they are both so happy they don't know how miserable they are. Motel keeps talking about a sewing machine. I know You're very busy —wars and revolutions, floods, plagues, all those little things that bring people to You — couldn't You take a second away from Your catastrophes and get it for him? How much trouble would it be? Oh, and while You're in the neighborhood, my horse's left leg — Am I bothering You too much? I'm sorry. As the Good Book says — Why should I tell You what the Good Book says? *(Exits.)*

SCENE ONE

The exterior of TEVYE's *house. Afternoon.* HODEL *enters, petulantly, followed by* PERCHIK.

PERCHIK
Please don't be upset, Hodel.

HODEL
Why should I be upset? If you must leave, you must.

PERCHIK

I do have to. They expect me in Kiev tomorrow morning.

HODEL

So you told me. Then goodbye.

PERCHIK

Great changes are about to take place in this country. Tremendous changes. But they can't happen by themselves.

HODEL

So naturally you feel that you personally have to —

PERCHIK

Not only me. Many people. Jews, Gentiles, many people hate what is going on. Don't you understand?

HODEL

I understand, of course. You want to leave. Then goodbye.

PERCHIK

Hodel, your father, the others here, think what happened at Tzeitel's wedding was a little cloudburst and it's over and everything will now be peaceful again. It won't. Horrible things are happening all over the land — pogroms, violence — whole villages are being emptied of their people. And it's reaching everywhere, and it will reach here. You understand?

HODEL

Yes, I — I suppose I do.

PERCHIK

I have work to do. The greatest work a man can do.

HODEL

Then goodbye, Perchik.

PERCHIK

Before I go (*he hesitates, then summons up courage*), there is a certain question I wish to discuss with you.

HODEL

Yes?

80

PERCHIK

A political question.

HODEL

What is it?

PERCHIK

The question of marriage.

HODEL

This is a political question?

PERCHIK

(Awkwardly)

In a theoretical sense, yes. The relationship between a man
and woman known as marriage is based on mutual beliefs, a
common attitude and philosophy towards society —

HODEL

And affection.

PERCHIK

And affection. This relationship has positive social values. It
reflects a unity and solidarity —

HODEL

And affection.

PERCHIK

Yes. And I personally am in favor of it. Do you understand?

HODEL

I think you are asking me to marry you.

PERCHIK

In a theoretical sense, yes, I am.

HODEL

I was hoping you were.

PERCHIK

Then I take it you approve? And we can consider ourselves engaged, even though I am going away? *(She nods.)* I am very
happy, Hodel. Very happy.

HODEL

So am I, Perchik.

81

PERCHIK

(Sings.)

["Now I Have Everything"]

I used to tell myself
That I had everything,
But that was only half true.
I had an aim in life,
And that was everything,
But now I even have you.

I have something that I would die for,
Someone that I can live for, too.

Yes, now I have everything —
Not only everything,
I have a little bit more —
Besides having everything,
I know what everything's for.

I used to wonder,
Could there be a wife
To share such a difficult, wand'ring kind of life.

HODEL

I was only out of sight,
Waiting right here.

PERCHIK

Who knows tomorrow
Where our home will be?

HODEL

I'll be with you and that's
Home enough for me.

PERCHIK

Everything is right at hand.

HODEL *and* PERCHIK

Simple and clear.

82

PERCHIK

I have something that I would die for,
Someone that I can live for, too.

Yes, now I have everything —
Not only everything,
I have a little bit more —
Besides having everything,
I know what everything's for.

HODEL

And when will we be married, Perchik?

PERCHIK

I will send for you as soon as I can. It will be a hard life, **Hodel**.

HODEL

But it will be less hard if we live it together.

PERCHIK

Yes.

(TEVYE *enters.*)

TEVYE

Good evening.

PERCHIK

Good evening. Reb Tevye, I have some bad news. I must leave this place.

TEVYE

When?

PERCHIK

Right away.

TEVYE

I'm sorry, Perchik. We will all miss you.

PERCHIK

But I also have some good news. You can congratulate me.

TEVYE

Congratulations. What for?

PERCHIK

We're engaged.

TEVYE

Engaged?

HODEL

Yes, Papa, we're engaged. (*Takes* PERCHIK's *hand*.)

TEVYE

(*Pleasantly, separating them*)

No, you're not. I know, you like him, and he likes you, but you're going away, and you're staying here, so have a nice trip, Perchik. I hope you'll be very happy, and my answer is no.

HODEL

Please, Papa, you don't understand.

TEVYE

I understand. I gave my permission to Motel and Tzeitel, so you feel that you also have a right. I'm sorry, Perchik. I like you, but you're going away, so go in good health and my answer is still no.

HODEL

You don't understand, Papa.

TEVYE

(*Patiently*)

You're not listening. I say no. I'm sorry, Hodel, but we'll find someone else for you, here in Anatevka.

PERCHIK

Reb Tevye.

TEVYE

What is it?

PERCHIK

We are not asking for your permission, only for your blessing. We are going to get married.

TEVYE

(*To* HODEL)

You're not asking for my permission?

84

But we would like your blessing, Papa.

TEVYE

["Tradition" Reprise]

I can't believe my own ears. My blessing? For What?
For going over my head? Impossible.
At least with Tzeitel and Motel, they asked me,
They begged me.
But now, if I like it or not,
She'll marry him.
So what do you want from me? Go on, be wed.
And tear out my beard and uncover my head.
Tradition!
They're not even asking permission
From the papa.
What's happening to the tradition?
One little time I pulled out a thread
And where has it led? Where has it led?

Where has it led? To this! A man tells me he is getting married.
He doesn't ask me, he tells me. But first, he abandons her.

HODEL

He is not abandoning me, Papa.

PERCHIK

As soon as I can, I will send for her and marry her. I love her.

TEVYE

(*Mimicking him*)

"I love her." Love. It's a new style. On the other hand, our
old ways were once new, weren't they? On the other hand.
they decided without parents, without a matchmaker. On the
other hand, did Adam and Eve have a matchmaker? Yes, they
did. Then it seems these two have the same matchmaker. (*Sings.*)

85

They're going over my head —
Unheard of, absurd.
For this they want to be blessed?—
Unthinkable.
I'll lock her up in her room.
I couldn't — I should! —
But look at my daughter's eyes.
She loves him.
Tradition!
(*Shrugs.*)

Very well, children, you have my blessing and my permission.

HODEL

Oh, thank you, Papa. You don't know how happy that makes me.

TEVYE

(*To the audience*)

What else could I do?

PERCHIK

Thank you, Papa.

TEVYE

(*Worried*)

"Thank you, Papa." What will I tell your mother? Another dream?

PERCHIK

Perhaps if you tell her something—that I am going to visit a rich uncle—something like that.

TEVYE

Please, Perchik. I can handle my own wife. (PERCHIK *and* HODEL *exit. He calls aggressively.*) Golde! Golde! (*She enters from the house. He speaks timidly.*) Hello, Golde. I've just been talking to Perchik and Hodel.

GOLDE

Well?

86

Villagers in bottle dance at Tzeitel's wedding

Beatrice Arthur and villagers—"I just heard"

TEVYE

They seem to be very fond of each other—

GOLDE

Well?

TEVYE

Well, I have decided to give them my permission to become engaged. (*Starts into the house.*)

GOLDE

(*Stopping him*)

What? Just like this? Without even asking me?

TEVYE

(*Roaring*)

Who asks you? I'm the father.

GOLDE

And who is he? A pauper. He has nothing, absolutely nothing!

TEVYE

(*Hesitating*)

I wouldn't say that. I hear he has a rich uncle, a very rich uncle. (*Changes the subject.*) He is a good man, Golde. I like him. He is a little crazy, but I like him. And what's more important, Hodel likes him. Hodel loves him. So what can we do? It's a new world, a new world. Love. (*Starts to go, then has a sudden thought.*) Golde — (*Sings.*)

["Do You Love Me?"]

Do you love me?

GOLDE

Do I what?

TEVYE

Do you love me?

GOLDE

Do I love you?
With our daughters getting married
And this trouble in the town,

87

You're upset, you're worn out,
Go inside, go lie down.
Maybe it's indigestion.

TEVYE

Golde, I'm asking you a question—

Do you love me?

GOLDE

You're a fool.

TEVYE

I know—

But do you love me?

GOLDE

Do I love you?
For twenty-five years I've washed your clothes,
Cooked your meals, cleaned your house,
Given you children, milked the cow.
After twenty-five years, why talk about
Love right now?

TEVYE

Golde, the first time I met you
Was on our wedding day.
I was scared.

GOLDE

I was shy.

TEVYE

I was nervous.

GOLDE

So was I.

TEVYE

But my father and my mother
Said we'd learn to love each other.
And now I'm asking, Golde,

Do you love me?

GOLDE

I'm your wife.

TEVYE

I know—

But do you love me?

GOLDE

Do I love him?
For twenty-five years I've lived with him,
Fought with him, starved with him.
Twenty-five years my bed is his.
If that's not love, what is?

TEVYE

Then you love me?

GOLDE

I suppose I do.

TEVYE

And I suppose I love you, too.

TEVYE *and* GOLDE

It doesn't change a thing,
But even so,
After twenty-five years,
It's nice to know.

SCENE TWO

The village street. YENTE, TZEITEL, *and other villagers cross.*
YENTE *and* TZEITEL *meet.)*

FISH SELLER

Fish! Fresh fish!

YENTE

Oh, Tzeitel, Tzeitel darling. Guess who I just saw! Your sister
Chava with that Fyedka! And it's not the first time I've seen
them together.

89

TZEITEL

You saw Chava with Fyedka?

YENTE

Would I make it up? Oh, and Tzeitel, I happened to be at the post office today and the postman told me there was a letter there for your sister Hodel.

TZEITEL

Wonderful, I'll go get it. (*Starts off.*)

YENTE

I got it! It's from her intended, Perchik. (*Hands letter to* TZEITEL.)

TZEITEL

Hodel will be so happy, she's been waiting — But it's open.

YENTE

It happened to be open. (TZEITEL *exits.* YENTE *watches her leave, then turns to a group of* VILLAGERS.) Rifka, I have such news for you.

["I Just Heard"]

Remember Perchik, that crazy student?
Remember at the wedding,
When Tzeitel married Motel
And Perchik started dancing
With Tevye's daughter Hodel?
Well, I just learned
That Perchik's been arrested, in Kiev.

VILLAGERS

No!

YENTE

Yes!

(YENTE *and the* FIRST GROUP *exit. A* WOMAN
crosses to a SECOND GROUP.)

90

Shandel, Shandel! Wait till I tell you —

> Remember Perchik, that crazy student?
> Remember at the wedding.
> He danced with Tevye's Hodel?
> Well,
> I just heard
> That Hodel's been arrested, in Kiev.

VILLAGERS
No! Terrible, terrible!

(The SECOND GROUP *exits. A* SECOND WOMAN *crosses to a* THIRD GROUP.)

SECOND WOMAN
Mirila!

> Do you remember Perchik,
> That student, from Kiev?
> Remember how he acted
> When Tzeitel married Motel?
> Well, I just heard
> That Motel's been arrested
> For dancing at the wedding.

VILLAGERS
No!

SECOND WOMAN
In Kiev!

(The THIRD GROUP *exits.* MENDEL *crosses to a* FOURTH GROUP.)

MENDEL
Rabbi! Rabbi!

> Remember Perchik, with all his strange ideas?

Remember Tzeitel's wedding
Where Tevye danced with Golde?
Well I just heard
That Tevye's been arrested
And Golde's gone to Kiev.

VILLAGERS
No!

MENDEL
God forbid.

VILLAGERS
She didn't.

MENDEL
She did.

(*The* FOURTH GROUP *exits.* AVRAM *crosses to the* FIFTH GROUP. YENTE *enters and stands at the edge of the* GROUP *to listen.*)

AVRAM
Listen, everybody, terrible news — terrible —

Remember Perchik,
Who started all the trouble?
Well, I just heard, from someone who should know,
That Golde's been arrested,
And Hodel's gone to Kiev.
Motel studies dancing,
And Tevye's acting strange.
Shprintze has the measles,
And Bielke has the mumps.

YENTE
And that's what comes from men and women dancing!

SCENE THREE

The exterior of the railroad station. Morning. HODEL *enters and walks over to a bench.* TEVYE *follows, carrying her suitcase.*

HODEL

You don't have to wait for the train, Papa. You'll be late for your customers.

TEVYE

Just a few more minutes. Is he in bad trouble, that hero of yours? *(She nods.)* Arrested? *(She nods.)* And convicted?

HODEL

Yes, but he did nothing wrong. He cares nothing for himself. Everything he does is for humanity.

TEVYE

But if he did nothing wrong, he wouldn't be in trouble.

HODEL

Papa, how can you say that, a learned man like you? What wrongs did Joseph do, and Abraham, and Moses? And they had troubles.

TEVYE

But why won't you tell me where he is now, this Joseph of yours?

HODEL

It is far, Papa, terribly far. He is in a settlement in Siberia.

TEVYE

Siberia! And he asks you to leave your father and mother and join him in that frozen wasteland, and marry him there?

HODEL

No, Papa, he did not ask me to go. I want to go. I don't want him to be alone. I want to help him in his work. It is the greatest work a man can do.

TEVYE

But, Hodel, baby —

Papa — (*Sings.*)

["Far From the Home I Love"]

How can I hope to make you understand
Why I do what I do,
Why I must travel to a distant land
Far from the home I love?

Once I was happily content to be
As I was, where I was,
Close to the people who are close to me
Here in the home I love.

Who could see that a man would come
Who would change the shape of my dreams?
Helpless, now, I stand with him
Watching older dreams grow dim.

Oh, what a melancholy choice this is,
Wanting home, wanting him,
Closing my heart to every hope but his,
Leaving the home I love.

There where my heart has settled long ago
I must go, I must go.
Who could imagine I'd be wand'ring so
Far from the home I love?
Yet, there with my love, I'm home.

TEVYE

And who, my child, will there be to perform a marriage, there
in the wilderness?

HODEL

Papa, I promise you, we will be married under a canopy.

94

TEVYE

No doubt a rabbi or two was also arrested. Well, give him my regards, this Moses of yours. I always thought he was a good man. Tell him I rely on his honor to treat my daughter well. Tell him that.

HODEL

Papa, God alone knows when we shall see each other again.

TEVYE

Then we will leave it in His hands. (*He kisses* HODEL, *starts to go, stops, looks back, then looks to heaven.*) Take care of her. See that she dresses warm. (*He exits, leaving* HODEL *seated on the station platform.*)

SCENE FOUR

The village street, some months later. The VILLAGERS *enter.*

AVRAM

Reb Mordcha, did you hear the news? A new arrival at Motel and Tzeitel's.

MORDCHA

A new arrival at Motel and Tzeitel's? I must congratulate him.

AVRAM

Rabbi, did you hear the news? A new arrival at Motel and Tzeitel's.

RABBI

Really?

MENDEL

Mazeltov.

FIRST MAN

Mazeltov.

SECOND MAN

Mazeltov.

(SHANDEL *crosses quickly, meeting a* WOMAN.)

95

WOMAN

Shandel, where are you running?

SHANDEL

To my boy, Motel. There's a new arrival there.

VILLAGERS

Mazeltov, Mazeltov, Mazeltov, Shandel.

SCENE FIVE

MOTEL'*s tailor shop.* MOTEL *and* CHAVA *are in the shop.*
GOLDE *and the* VILLAGERS *crowd around* MOTEL*, congratulating*
him. They fall back, revealing a used sewing machine.

VILLAGERS

Mazeltov, Motel. We just heard. Congratulations. Wonderful.

MOTEL

Thank you, thank you, very much.

(TZEITEL *enters.*)

AVRAM

Mazeltov, Tzeitel.

TZEITEL
(Ecstatic)

You got it!

MOTEL

I got it!

TZEITEL

It's beautiful.

MOTEL

I know!

TZEITEL

Have you tried it yet?

MOTEL
(Holds up two different-colored
pieces of cloth sewn together.)

Look.

TZEITEL

Beautiful.

MOTEL

I know. And in less than a minute. And see how close and even the stitches are.

TZEITEL

Beautiful.

MOTEL

I know. From now on, my clothes will be perfect, made by machine. No more handmade clothes.

(*The* RABBI *enters.*)

MORDCHA

The rabbi, the rabbi.

MOTEL

Look, Rabbi, my new sewing machine.

RABBI

Mazeltov.

TZEITEL

Rabbi, is there a blessing for a sewing machine?

RABBI

There is a blessing for everything. (*Prays.*) Amen.

VILLAGERS

Amen. . . . Mazeltov. (VILLAGERS, RABBI *exit.*)

GOLDE

And the baby? How is the baby?

TZEITEL

He's wonderful, Mama.

(FYEDKA *enters. There is an awkward pause.*)

FYEDKA

Good afternoon.

MOTEL

Good afternoon, Fyedka.

FYEDKA

I came for the shirt.

MOTEL

It's ready.

TZEITEL

See, it's my new sewing machine.

FYEDKA

I see. Congratulations.

MOTEL

Thank you.

FYEDKA
                    (*After another awkward moment*)
Good day. (*Leaves the shop.*)

MOTEL

Good day.

GOLDE

How does it work?

MOTEL

See, it's an amazing thing. You work it with your foot and your
hand.

> (CHAVA *exits from the shop and meets*
> FYEDKA *outside.*)

FYEDKA

They still don't know about us? (*She shakes her head.*) You
must tell them.

CHAVA

I will, but I'm afraid.

FYEDKA

Chava, let me talk to your father.

CHAVA

No, that would be the worst thing, I'm sure of it.

FYEDKA

Let me try.

CHAVA

No, I'll talk to him. I promise.

(TEVYE *enters.*)

FYEDKA
(Extending his hand)

Good afternoon.

TEVYE
(Takes the hand limply.)

Good afternoon.

FYEDKA
(Looks at CHAVA)

Good day. *(Exits.)*

TEVYE

Good day. What were you and he talking about?

CHAVA

Nothing, we were just talking. (TEVYE *turns to go into* MOTEL'S *shop.)* Papa, Fyedka and I have known each other for a long time and and —

TEVYE
(Turning back)

Chava, I would be much happier if you would remain friends from a distance. You must not forget who you are and who that man is.

CHAVA

He has a name, Papa.

TEVYE

Of course. All creatures on earth have a name.

CHAVA

Fyedka is not a creature, Papa. Fyedka is a man.

99

TEVYE

Who says that he isn't? It's just that he is a different kind of man. As the Good Book says, "Each shall seek his own kind." Which, translated, means, "A bird may love a fish, but where would they build a home together?" (*He starts toward the shop, but* CHAVA *seizes his arm.*)

CHAVA

The world is changing, Papa.

TEVYE

No. Some things do not change for us. Some things will never change.

CHAVA

We don't feel that way.

TEVYE

We?

CHAVA

Fyedka and I. We want to be married.

TEVYE

Are you out of your mind? Don't you know what this means, marrying outside of the faith?

CHAVA

But, Papa —

TEVYE

No, Chava! I said no! Never talk about this again! Never mention his name again! Never see him again! Never! Do you understand me?

CHAVA

Yes, Papa. I understand you.

> (GOLDE *enters from the shop, followed by* SHPRINTZE *and* BIELKE.)

GOLDE

You're finally here? Let's go home. It's time for supper.

100

TEVYE

I want to see Motel's new machine.

GOLDE

You'll see it some other time. It's late.

TEVYE

Quiet, woman, before I get angry. And when I get angry, even flies don't dare to fly.

GOLDE

I'm very frightened of you. After we finish supper, I'll faint. Come home.

TEVYE

(Sternly)

Golde. I am the man in the family. I am head of the house. I want to see Motel's new machine, now! (Strides to the door of the shop, opens it, looks in, closes the door, turns to GOLDE.) Now, let's go home! (They exit. CHAVA remains looking after them.)

SCENE SIX

A road. Late afternoon. TEVYE is pushing his cart.

TEVYE

(Sinks down on the cart.)

How long can that miserable horse of mine complain about his leg? (Looks up.) Dear God, if I can walk on two legs, why can't he walk on three? I know I shouldn't be too upset with him. He is one of Your creatures and he has the same rights as I have: the right to be sick, the right to be hungry, the right to work like a horse. And, dear God, I'm sick and tired of pulling this cart. I know, I know, I should push it a while. (He starts pushing the cart.)

GOLDE

(Offstage)

Tevye! (She enters, upset.) Tevye!

TEVYE
(*Struck by her manner*)

What? What is it?

GOLDE

It's Chava. She left home this morning. With Fyedka.

TEVYE

What?

GOLDE

I looked all over for her. I even went to the priest. He told me
— they were married.

TEVYE

Married! (*She nods.*) Go home, Golde. We have other children at home. Go home, Golde. You have work to do. I have
work to do.

GOLDE

But, Chava —

TEVYE

Chava is dead to us! We will forget her. Go home. (GOLDE
exits. TEVYE *sings.*)

["Chavaleh"]

TEVYE

Little bird, little Chavaleh,
I don't understand what's happening today.
Everything is all a blur.
All I can see is a happy child,
The sweet little bird you were,
Chavaleh, Chavaleh.

Little bird, little Chavaleh,
You were always such a pretty little thing.
Everybody's fav'rite child,
Gentle and kind and affectionate,
What a sweet little bird you were,
Chavaleh, Chavaleh.

102

(CHAVA *enters.*)

CHAVA

Papa, I want to talk with you. Papa, stop. At least listen to me. Papa, I beg you to accept us.

TEVYE

(*To heaven*)

Accept them? How can I accept them. Can I deny everything I believe in? On the other hand, can I deny my own child? On the other hand, how can I turn my back on my faith, my people? If I try to bend that far, I will break. On the other hand . . . there is no other hand. No Chava. No — no — no!

CHAVA

Papa. Papa.

VILLAGERS

(*Seen behind a transparent curtain, sing as* CHAVA *exits slowly.*)

Tradition. Tradition. Tradition.

SCENE SEVEN

TEVYE's *barn.* YENTE *enters with two* BOYS, *teenage students, who are obviously uncomfortable in the situation.*

YENTE

Golde, are you home? I've got the two boys, the boys I told you about.

(GOLDE *enters, followed by* SHPRINTZE *and* BIELKE.)

Golde darling, here they are, wonderful boys, both learned boys, Golde, from good families, each of them a prize, a jewel. You couldn't do better for your girls — just right. From the top of the tree.

GOLDE

I don't know, Yente. My girls are still so young.

YENTE

So what do they look like, grandfathers? Meanwhile they'll be

103

engaged, nothing to worry about later, no looking around, their future all signed and sealed.

GOLDE

Which one for which one?

YENTE

What's the difference? Take your pick.

GOLDE

I don't know, Yente. I'll have to talk with —

(*Enter* LAZAR WOLF, AVRAM, MENDEL, MORDCHA, *and other* VILLAGERS.)

AVRAM

Golde, is Reb Tevye home?

GOLDE

Yes, but he's in the house. Why, is there some trouble?

AVRAM

(*To* BIELKE *and* SHPRINTZE)

Call your father. (*They exit.*)

YENTE

(*To the* BOYS)

Go home. Tell your parents I'll talk to them. (*They exit.*)

GOLDE

What is it? Why are you all gathered together like a bunch of goats? What's —

(TEVYE *enters.*)

AVRAM

Reb Tevye, have you seen the constable today?

TEVYE

No. Why?

LAZAR

There are some rumors in town. We thought because you knew him so well, maybe he told you what is true and what is not.

What rumors?

AVRAM

Someone from Zolodin told me that there was an edict issued in St. Petersburg that all — Shh. shh.

(*He stops as the* CONSTABLE *enters with* TWO MEN.)

TEVYE

Welcome, your Honor. What's the good news in the world?

CONSTABLE

I see you have company.

TEVYE

They are my friends.

CONSTABLE

It's just as well. What I have to say is for their ears also. Tevye, how much time do you need to sell your house and all your household goods? (*There is a gasp from the* VILLAGERS. *They are stunned. They look to* TEVYE.)

TEVYE

Why should I sell my house? Is it in anybody's way?

CONSTABLE

I came here to tell you that you are going to have to leave Anatevka.

TEVYE

And how did I come to deserve such an honor?

CONSTABLE

Not just you, of course, but all of you. At first I thought you might be spared, Tevye, because of your daughter Chava, who married —

TEVYE

My daughter is dead!

CONSTABLE

I understand. At any rate, it affects all of you. You have to leave.

105

TEVYE

But this corner of the world has always been our home. Why should we leave?

CONSTABLE
(Irritated)

I don't know why. There's trouble in the world. Troublemakers.

TEVYE
(Ironically)

Like us!

CONSTABLE

You aren't the only ones. Your people must leave all the villages — Zolodin, Rabalevka. The whole district must be emptied. *(Horrified and amazed exclamations from the VILLAGERS.)* I have an order here, and it says that you must sell your homes and be out of here in three days.

VILLAGERS

Three days! . . . Out in three days!

TEVYE

And you who have known us all your life, you'd carry out this order?

CONSTABLE

I have nothing to do with it, don't you understand?

TEVYE
(Bitterly)

We understand.

FIRST MAN

And what if we refuse to go?

CONSTABLE

You will be forced out.

LAZAR

We will defend ourselves.

VILLAGERS

Stay in our homes . . . Refuse to leave . . . Keep our land.

106

SECOND MAN

Fight!

CONSTABLE

Against our army? I wouldn't advise it!

TEVYE

I have some advice for you. Get off my land! (*The* VILLAGERS *crowd toward the* CONSTABLE *and his* MEN.) This is still my home, my land. Get off my land! (*The* CONSTABLE *and his men start to go. The* CONSTABLE *turns.*)

CONSTABLE

You have three days! (*Exits.*)

FIRST MAN

After a lifetime, a piece of paper and get thee out.

MORDCHA

We should get together with the people of Zolodin. Maybe they have a plan.

FIRST MAN

We should defend ourselves. An eye for an eye, a tooth for a tooth.

TEVYE

Very good. And that way, the whole world will be blind and toothless.

MENDEL

Rabbi, we've been waiting for the Messiah all our lives. Wouldn't this be a good time for him to come?

RABBI

We'll have to wait for him someplace else. Meanwhile, let's start packing. (*The* VILLAGERS *start to go, talking together.*)

VILLAGERS

He's right. . . . I'll see you before I go.

FIRST MAN

Three days!

MORDCHA

How will I be able to sell my shop? My merchandise?

THIRD MAN

Where can I go with a wife, her parents, and three children?

(*Exit all but* YENTE, GOLDE, AVRAM, LAZAR, MENDEL, *and* TEVYE.)

YENTE

Well, Anatevka hasn't been exactly the Garden of Eden.

AVRAM

That's true.

GOLDE

After all, what've we got here?   (*Sings.*)

["Anatevka"]

A little bit of this,
A little bit of that,

YENTE

A pot,

LAZAR

A pan,

MENDEL

A broom,

AVRAM

A hat.

TEVYE

Someone should have set a match to this place long ago.

MENDEL

A bench,

AVRAM

A tree,

GOLDE

So what's a stove?

LAZAR

Or a house?

MENDEL
(*Speaks.*)
People who pass through Anatevka don't even know they've been here.

GOLDE
A stick of wood,
YENTE
A piece of cloth.
ALL
What do we leave?
Nothing much,
Only Anatevka. . . .

Anatevka, Anatevka,
Underfed, overworked Anatevka,
Where else could Sabbath be so sweet?

Anatevka, Anatevka
Intimate, obstinate Anatevka,
Where I know everyone I meet.

Soon I'll be a stranger in a strange new place,
Searching for an old familiar face
From Anatevka.

I belong in Anatevka,
Tumbledown, workaday Anatevka,
Dear little village, little town of mine.

GOLDE
Eh, it's just a place.
MENDEL
And our forefathers have been forced out of many, many places at a moment's notice.
TEVYE
(*Shrugs.*)
Maybe that's why we always wear our hats.

SCENE EIGHT

Outside TEVYE's *house.* MOTEL *and* TZEITEL *are packing baggage into a cart and a wagon.* SHPRINTZE *and* BIELKE *enter with bundles.*

SHPRINTZE

Where will we live in America?

MOTEL

With Uncle Abram, but he doesn't know it yet.

SHPRINTZE

I wish you and the baby were coming with us.

TZEITEL

We'll be staying in Warsaw until we have enough money to join you.

GOLDE

(Entering, with goblets)

Motel, be careful with these. My mother and father, may they rest in peace, gave them to us on our wedding day.

TZEITEL

(To BIELKE *and* SHPRINTZE*)*

Come, children, help me pack the rest of the clothes. *(They exit into house.)*

YENTE

(Enters)

Golde darling, I had to see you before I left because I have such news for you. Golde darling, you remember I told you yesterday I didn't know where to go, what to do with these old bones? Now I know! You want to hear? I'll tell you. Golde darling, all my life I've dreamed of going to one place and now I'll walk, I'll crawl, I'll get there. Guess where. You'll never guess. Every year at Passover, what do we say? "Next year in Jerusalem, next year in the Holy Land."

110

GOLDE
You're going to the Holy Land!

YENTE

You guessed! And you know why? In my sleep, my husband, my Aaron, came to me and said, "Yente, go to the Holy Land." Usually, of course, I wouldn't listen to him, because, good as he was, too much brains he wasn't blessed with. But in my sleep it's a sign. Right? So, somehow or other, I'll get to the Holy Land. And you want to know what I'll do there? I'm a matchmaker, no? I'll arrange marriages, yes? Children come from marriages, no? So I'm going to the Holy Land to help our people increase and multiply. It's my mission. So goodbye, Golde.

GOLDE

Goodbye, Yente. Be well and go in peace. (*They embrace.*)

YENTE

(*Exiting*)

Maybe next time, Golde, we will meet on happier occasions. Meanwhile, we suffer, we suffer, we suffer in silence! Right? Of course, right. (*She exits.* GOLDE *sits on a large straw trunk, sadly wrapping a pair of silver goblets.* TEVYE *enters, carrying a bundle of books, and puts them on the wagon.*)

TEVYE

We'll have to hurry, Golde. (*She is looking at the goblets.*) Come, Golde, we have to leave soon.

GOLDE

Leave. It sounds so easy.

TEVYE

We'll all be together soon. Motel, Tzeitel and the baby, they'll come too, you'll see. That Motel is a person.

GOLDE

And Hodel and Perchik? When will we ever see them?

111

TEVYE

Do they come visiting us from Siberia every Sabbath? You know what she writes. He sits in prison, and she works, and soon he will be set free and together they will turn the world upside down. She couldn't be happier. And the other children will be with us.

GOLDE
(*Quietly*)

Not all.

TEVYE
(*Sharply*)

All. Come, Golde, we have to get finished.

GOLDE

I still have to sweep the floor.

TEVYE

Sweep the floor?

GOLDE

I don't want to leave a dirty house. (*She exits behind the house as* LAZAR *enters, carrying a large suitcase.*)

LAZAR

Well, Tevye, I'm on my way.

TEVYE

Where are you going?

LAZAR

Chicago. In America. My wife, Fruma-Sarah, may she rest in peace, has a brother there.

TEVYE

That's nice.

LAZAR

I hate him, but a relative is a relative! (*They embrace.*) Good-bye, Tevye. (LAZAR *exits.* TEVYE *enters the house, passing* TZEITEL, *who enters with a blanket and a small bundle.*)

TEVYE

Tzeitel, are they finished inside?

TZEITEL

Almost, Papa. (TZEITEL *puts the blanket on* MOTEL's *wagon, kneels down, and begins rummaging in the bundle.* CHAVA *and* FYEDKA *enter.* TZEITEL *turns to enter the house, and sees them.*) Chava! (CHAVA *runs to her. They embrace.* TZEITEL *looks toward the house.*) Papa will see you.

CHAVA

I want him to. I want to say goodbye to him.

TZEITEL

He will not listen.

CHAVA

But at least he will hear.

TZEITEL

Maybe it would be better if I went inside and told Mama that —

(GOLDE *comes round the side of the house.*)

GOLDE

Chava!

(*She starts toward her as* TEVYE *enters from the house with a length of rope. He sees them, turns, re-enters house, returns, and bends down to tie up the straw trunk, his back to* CHAVA *and* FYEDKA.)

CHAVA

Papa, we came to say goodbye. (TEVYE *does not respond, but goes on working.*) We are also leaving this place. We are going to Cracow.

FYEDKA

We cannot stay among people who can do such things to others.

113

CHAVA

We wanted you to know that. Goodbye, Papa, Mama. *(She waits for an answer, gets none, and turns to go.)*

FYEDKA

Yes, we are also moving. Some are driven away by edicts, others by silence. Come, Chava.

TZEITEL

Goodbye, Chava, Fyedka.

TEVYE

(To TZEITEL, *prompting her under his breath as he turns to another box)*

God be with you!

TZEITEL

(Looks at him, then speaks to Chava, gently.)

God be with you!

CHAVA

We will write to you in America. If you like.

GOLDE

We will be staying with Uncle Abram.

CHAVA

Yes, Mama. *(*CHAVA *and* FYEDKA *exit.* TEVYE *turns and watches them leave. There is a moment of silence; then he turns on* GOLDE.*)*

TEVYE

(With mock irritation)

We will be staying with Uncle Abram! We will be staying with Uncle Abram! The whole world has to know our business!

GOLDE

Stop yelling and finish packing. We have a train to catch.

*(*MOTEL, SHPRINTZE, *and* BIELKE *enter from the house.)*

TEVYE

I don't need your advice, Golde. Tzeitel, don't forget the baby.

114

We have to catch a train, and a boat. Bielke, Shprintze, put
the bundles on the wagon.

> (TEVYE *moves the wagon to the center
> of the stage, and* MOTEL *puts the trunk
> on it.* TZEITEL *brings the baby out of the
> house. They turn to one another for
> goodbyes.*)

TZEITEL

Goodbye, Papa. (*They embrace.*)

GOLDE

Goodbye, Motel.

MOTEL

Goodbye, Mama.

> (TZEITEL *and* GOLDE *embrace.*)

TEVYE

Work hard, Motel. Come to us soon.

MOTEL

I will, Reb Tevye. I'll work hard. (TEVYE *takes one last look
at the baby, then* TZEITEL *and* MOTEL *exit with their cart. When
they are gone,* TEVYE *turns to the wagon.*)

TEVYE
(*Picking up pots*)

Come, children. Golde, we can leave these pots.

GOLDE

No, we can't.

TEVYE

All right, we'll take them. (*Puts them back.*)

BIELKE
(*Childishly, swinging around with* SHPRINTZE)

We're going on a train and a boat. We're going on a —

GOLDE

(Sharply)

Stop that! Behave yourself! We're not in America yet!

TEVYE

Come, children. Let's go.

> *(The stage begins to revolve, and* TEVYE *begins to pull the wagon in the opposite direction. The other* VIL- LAGERS, *including the* FIDDLER, *join the circle. The revolve stops. There is a last moment together, and the* VILLAGERS *exit, at different times and in opposite directions, leaving the family on stage.* TEVYE *begins to pull his wagon upstage, revealing the* FIDDLER, *playing his theme.* TEVYE *stops, turns, beckons to him. The* FIDDLER *tucks his violin under his arm and follows the family upstage as the curtain falls.)*

116